T0149324

MEMORIES
OF AN
AMERICAN LIFE

TRUE STORIES FROM THE EARLY 1900S
OF A LARGE FAMILY IN A SMALL INDIANA TOWN

JULIAN K. NAIL

authorHOUSE®

AuthorHouse™
1663 Liberty Drive
Bloomington, IN 47403
www.authorhouse.com
Phone: 1 (800) 839-8640

Published by AuthorHouse   03/19/2016

ISBN: 978-1-5049-8510-9 (sc)
ISBN: 978-1-5049-8511-6(hc)
ISBN: 978-1-5049-8512-3 (e)

Library of Congress Control Number: 2016904311

Print information available on the last page.

CONTENTS

Dedicated to the memory of my wonderful parents,
Sherman A. and Mary Alice (Burgett) Nail

And to the memory of my beautiful West Virginia bride,
Betty L. (Satterfield) Nail

Another book by J.K. Nail

WWII: Remembrances, Observations, Perspectives

Rio Norte Press 2010

ACKNOWLEDGEMENTS

I am indebted to several people who helped with the development of this book.

Once I completed the hand-written recording of my stories, Teresa Fales, Christopher Fales, Alexandria Maitlen, and Beverly McConnell converted my chicken scratching into type-written pages. And that wasn't easy. Even I struggle sometimes trying figure out what those collection of letters intended to be legible words actually say. For their diligent dedication in assisting me, I am grateful.

Once the pages started resembling a manuscript, Sue Quinlan did some proof reading / pre-editing for me, which began the process of transforming a collection of stories into an actual book. Thank you, Sue.

Kathleen Marusak, my editor, modestly proclaimed that she did little more than polish my writing. But the truth is she took the manuscript to a professional level that would never have been realized without her. What is most special about Ms. Marusak's approach to editing is that she is intent on maintaining the writer's voice, which was very important to me. You know how much I appreciate you, Kathleen.

My good friends Jim Key and Bryan Martinez helped with the artistic elements. Bryan designed the cover. Both Bryan and Jim worked their magic on the photo section, scanning and tweaking photographs that date back as far as the early 1900s. Speaking of photos, several persons helped me round-up pictures from days gone by. My nieces Nancy Molitor and

Leah Willman provided some valued contributions as did my nephew, Dick Judy, and my cousin, Mary Jane Rose. I count it a blessing that the St. Paul, Indiana historian, Gladys Pike happens to be a long-time friend, and that she, too, was kind enough to help with the photo collection.

I could never have completed this project without a great deal of behind-the-scenes assistance on the home front from my good friends John and Jeanne Henry. I am indebted to them for believing in the book and helping me complete all the many steps to publication.

As is noted in the introduction, my nephew, Jim Steiner was the one who actually put me on the quest to publish a book about my parents. The entire Nail clan – past, present, and future – is indebted to you, Jim.

Mary Jane Rose, a cousin whom I've always considered one of my closest friends, was among the many relatives who regularly nudged me with gentle reminders to stay the course. At recent family reunions, two questions came from all my wonderful nieces, nephews, etc. "How are you?" and "How's the book coming?" I considered your constant reminders votes of confidence. A heart-felt thanks to all of you for your ongoing support and encouragement. I sincerely appreciate it.

INTRODUCTION

Memories do have a place to begin and I guess James Nail Steiner's request is as good as any. Jim is my youngest nephew. He asked if I would record some of the stories I could remember about his grandparents. I am the youngest and last of seven children. I have three brothers and three sisters, all deceased. Some folks would call them siblings, but not me. I prefer the terms brothers and sisters. Sure, we all came from the same root stock, but we were all as different as the myriad flakes in a snowstorm.

Our parents were born in the third quarter of the 19th century: Dad, November 27, 1871; Mother, September 23, 1874. Johnson County records show that Dad married Matilda Burns in 1891. They had an infant March 12, 1892. The mother and the infant died in the typhoid epidemic. As the last child, I would be the least likely one to know the specifics. Like most people, curiosity did not pay a visit until after the folks who could answer the questions were long gone. Lick Spring or Mt. Comfort cemeteries might turn up grave markers to anyone caring to look.

I do recall Mother mentioning that her oldest brother, Dillard Alonzo Burgett, MD, was also a casualty of the epidemic. He died on October 22, 1893. Mother was adamant. Faithful Dillard was working long hours in the cure of the sick, working too hard doing his duties. He was not eating properly or in a timely manner, missing meals, always on the go with little or no help, faithful to his calling.

It was on the 13th day of August, 1902 that my father, Sherman A. Nail, and my mother, Mary Alice Burgett, were married. That was the point in time when the stories you are about to read began to form. What follows are remembrances, observations and perspectives of my parents, our family and the St. Paul, Indiana community in which we lived.

As a young boy I sensed that my dad and my mother were excellent parents. And, as an employee in Dad's store, I always thought of him as someone who was exceptionally good with customers and not overly consumed with making a profit. Dad was a service-oriented businessman long before the term became a point of discussion in university classrooms. But it wasn't until later in my life that I came to appreciate just how special Mom and Dad were as parents—and how exceptional Sherman Nail was as a store owner. Once I saw what was considered the norm in both the family and business environments, I realized how extraordinary my exposure to family and business had been. The longer I reflected upon the amazing experiences I had as a boy and a young man in St. Paul, Indiana, the more certain I became that the stories about these glory days of my parents should be shared.

HISTORY AND BACKGROUND OF SHERMAN, MARY ALICE AND OTHER FAMILY MEMBERS

FIRST NAMES, GENERALLY SPEAKING

The Civil War (1861-1865) had ended five years, seven months before Dad's birth, November 27, 1871. Patriotic fervor still ran high in rural Johnson County. The midwife who assisted in the delivery of two baby boys also suggested names for the boys. The Smythers named their son Grant, and the Nails chose Sherman.

Perhaps it was inevitable; Grant and Sherman were inseparable friends, playmates, and schoolmates. Dad always spoke highly of Grant. An unparalleled camaraderie existed between the two as though they shared a great trust. Apparently Dad's moving his family to St. Paul had no ill effect on the friendship. Dad's brothers were the likely relays between Grant and Sherman. Since Dad's drivability was confined to a span of mares in front of a red-wheeled buggy, his radius of travel was quite limited. Don't ask me. I never saw Dad drive anything. A cousin has made a diligent effort to get information about Grant, to no avail.

UNCOMMON NAMES WERE COMMONPLACE

As far as masculine names go, Dad was luckier than his two brothers. Dad's first brother was named Gova, pronounced Govee. No one in the present-day family knows from whence that name came. Perhaps of

German descent Henry or John, or maybe a hand-me-down German family name. The youngest son was named Perington. I think Dad's mother, of Welsh descent, may have contributed that name. When Perington was of legal age, he changed his name to Purton.

It must have been tradition. Uncle Gova and Aunt Ouvey laid ringers on their two sons, Wendolyn and Leighton Temple. Wendolyn officially changed his name to Wendol. His niece, at an early age, could not roll her tongue around Wendol, so to his little niece he was Uncle Winnie. Wendol's kid brother died when he was four years old.

FAMILY NAMES

Death seemed to be a constant companion to homesteaders, especially children. Emma Louella was born August 25, 1872, twenty-three months before our own mother, and died at age five in 1877. Mom and Sarah Ethel (Aunt Sadie, March 27, 1883–December 18, 1977) talked often about the death of their little sister. Mom had mourned the death of Emma as though she were her baby sister, when in fact she was born before Mom, as I learned later when reading the Burgett genealogy book.

WILLIAMSON

Mother lamented the loss of a cousin, sixteen-year-old Williamson, August 2, 1840-October 12, 1859, although he died long before Mother was born. Will was currycombing a horse in a box stall. There was a loud clap of thunder above the barn stall. The horse reared up in the narrow box stall and thrashed about, kicking young Will in the head. A bright, smart, ambitious young man, he never recovered from the tragic accident. He is buried in Lick Spring Cemetery.

AUNT NANNY ANN

Aunt Nanny Ann, February 16, 1877–November 9, 1942, married Edgil Hemphill on November 6, 1895. I don't know whether Nanny was her given name, but that is what everyone called her and Nanny is on her grave marker in the Franklin Cemetery. I think Uncle Edgil may have been in the building trades. I was in the barn looking for something in a trunk behind Aunt Nanny's house, a picture Aunt Nanny wanted. When I opened the trunk, I saw it contained a WWI Army uniform. It could have been Uncle Elmer's. If Edgil served in WWI, no one ever mentioned it.

STUDENT AND TEACHER

Dad liked to read. With help from his mother, more than likely he taught himself how to read. He had an insatiable appetite for the printed word. Perhaps the family Bible was one of his textbooks. Dad recalled reading about the Indian wars in the West. He read of Brevet General Custer's last stand at Little Bighorn in 1876. Dad attended school in Trafalgar and graduated from high school there. The school board convinced Sherman to take two months' Normal Training so he could become a school teacher, which he did, so he could teach the next school year. Many two-year Normal Trained School Teachers were still teaching grade school students into the 1950s when the school teacher requirements were revised to require a Bachelor's degree immediately for beginning teachers plus a Master's degree within five years.

Dad had one prize pupil with whom he kept in contact. His surname was Richardson, a fairly large family in that area. The pupil earned a scholarship to Indiana University and I think Dad said he remained at

Indiana University on their teaching staff after his graduation at the top of his class. Hard work never hurts anyone, whatever form it takes.

Dad may have started in 1880 in a one-room schoolhouse. Dad taught Mother's youngest sister and she praised him for it.

Sadie bragged about what a good teacher Dad was when he taught school in the Hensley Township school system.

CO-OP MANAGER

Dad never went back to his farming roots after teaching. He became the manager of the Farmer's Cooperative. The Co-op had everything the members needed and Dad kept the inventory at the proper levels. The Co-op was near the railroad siding because if bought in carload lots, the price of the merchandise was less expensive.

Dad was rather independent. Perhaps he wanted to go into business for himself. The Farmers' Cooperative was successful but the profits of his enterprise, as the Co-op intended, went to the farmer stockholders. How Dad found out about the general merchandise store in St. Paul is on my part speculation. Perhaps a drummer that sold merchandise to both businesses alerted Dad of the general merchandise store up for sale in St. Paul.

Dad persuaded his brother Gova, pronounced Govee, and brother-in-law, Carl Burgett, to go in on the purchase of the St. Paul business. They moved from Johnson County in November, 1918. I think Gova stayed another year or two, then went back home to build his carpenter business. Carl was a born salesman too. One of his first jobs was working for Garland Mill in Greensburg, Indiana. They produced, under their label, flour, corn meal, chicken and animal feed.

Dad was a shrewd businessman, buying boxcar loads of merchandise when practical. My sister Marian remembered boxcar loads of apples, sold at a discount prices directly from the boxcar on a RR siding across the street from the store. I, too, remember some of Dad's car-load purchases. I think Dad conducted the negotiations when buying the business. Unlike now, in those days, a handshake was binding. Barley, the merchant who sold the business, in a rock-solid binding handshake, told Dad and his partners that if he ever decided to go back into competition, he would wait a full year before doing so. Dad got a prime lesson in a good-faith handshake. His competitor opened his new store in a vacant storeroom two doors from Dad's store within six months. So much for such a sissy weak handshake.

The store seemed to have more potential than their Trafalgar store. Dad was the oldest of the three Nail young men. Uncle Gova told me that Dad was the member of the family that convinced his brothers to George up the family name from the drab Nail to Naile. They all complied.

Uncle Perton stayed in Trafalgar with the store and Dad, Govee, and Uncle Carl, Mother's brother, went to the new store. Dad had arranged the purchase of the St. Paul store for the three partners.

FROM TRAFALGAR TO ST. PAUL

Late in 1918, Dad moved his family from Trafalgar to St. Paul, Decatur County. He and his partners, brother Gova and brother-in-law Carl Burgett, who had brought their families, had purchased Barley's General selling merchandise, clothing, shoes, and canned food. They were anxious to inventory the stock and get to work. Within two years, Dad had bought out his partners.

Moving to St. Paul, Dad brought his wife, five school-age children and a six-month-old infant. I do not know in what year between 1920 and 1928 this took place. 1923 was the year of my birth. Dad was on his own as the sole proprietor of the business. He would hire local women and men as clerks. When I got old enough, I remember Olive Cox and Roe Whiteinger who worked there, fine friends and employees.

HOW CAN I HELP YOU?

Dad was a born salesman. I think my brother James emulated Dad's persona. Dad or James sized up the purchase of a single-item encounter with a buyer. Dress shoes encouraged new dress socks or nylon hose for the ladies.

A farmer in to buy a new pair of Ball Band rubber boots for winter's cold rains, snow, and deep icy mud caused these salesmen to conjure up thick-knit wool socks and heavy felt boot liners. Dad kept both items at hand as an encouragement to the buyer. Rubber does not generate heat nor retain that which is within the boot, without help. The temperature within is governed by what the wearer is creating.

Into this environment I was thrust at a young age. Dad and James thrived on the challenge. I sold as best I could, following in their footsteps for that was what was expected of me, but I knew it could not possibly be my lifetime occupation. When the way out materialized, I hopped on board and never looked back. But that came later.

If it was shoes, then it was new socks, stockings or hose, depending on the gender. Dry goods for an apron or dress called for matching thread, bias binding tape, and lace trim.

After a time Uncle Gova returned to Trafalgar. Uncle Carl had no trouble finding good jobs. He sold flour, cornmeal, chicken mash and feed. His territory encompassed southern Indiana, part of Kentucky, Tennessee, Alabama, Georgia. He worked for Garland Mill in Greensburg. Uncle Carl, on his way home, stopping in Georgia, passed a watermelon field where harvesting was underway. Uncle Carl asked how the melons were running. The farmer picked out a nice-size melon, laid it on a burlap sack and drove the heel of his shoe into the melon. The melon split wide open. Uncle Carl started to pick up a piece of the rind. The farmer sliced off a big piece of the heart. "Here's how you taste how good a melon is." Uncle Carl loaded his touring car with melons to bring home. Dad sold them in the store.

DIRT FARMERS

When Dad uprooted his Johnson County family and brought them to St. Paul, he found you can take some of the dirt out of a dirt farmer, but don't try to take the farmer out of the dirt. I don't know how much of a garden they had in St. Paul, but I'd guess Mom had a hand in expanding it. When I was old enough to help, Mom found another patch of dirt that she and I could turn into growing space for parsnips, turnips, and greens.

PERSONAL EXPERIENCE STORIES AND NOTES (FROM CHILDHOOD THROUGH THE END OF WWII)

APPENDECTOMY ON THE KITCHEN TABLE

Uncle Will and Aunt Dolly had two sons, William and Robert. Sixteen-year-old William was very sick that Saturday morning. He was in great pain in the right side of his abdomen about a cupped hand's length from his navel. This was not an upset stomach. This was the era when doctors made house calls, and the doctor came and examined the teenager. "Clear the table. Put a heavy quilt on it covered with a clean sheet," the doctor demanded. "William has appendicitis; I need to operate right now. Will, boil water, lots of it. No time to get him to the hospital. Dolly, you will assist me." Aunt Dolly, always jolly, the practical joker, usually full of laughter, now revealed the hidden steel of her character. She could administer the chloroform, sop the blood, pass the instruments, and wipe the doctor's brow. This was her son. The appendix had burst, spreading the poison throughout his system. Young William died on that operating table in the dining room.

CATFISH FROM THE STONE QUARRY POND

I remember when Billy Alter and I went fishing in the stone quarry pond in Low Town. The pond was almost mudded-in from spring Flat

Rock River floods. We caught 50 or 60 pan-size catfish. Billy's mom said she would fry the fish for us if we would clean them. We had a washtub and Mrs. Alter boiled water. With a well-placed knife the catfish was dispatched of life. We dropped them into the tub. If you have ever peeled beets, that is the way that the catfish skin peeled away from the flesh. Further cleaning was a snap. 'Twas a powerful good catfish dinner. You just can't miss, with corn meal and catfish.

THE AROMA OF BURNING WOOD

In the winter, you didn't have to walk very far in St. Paul to know what kind of fuel was being burned to warm the houses. Wood was plentiful and cut in the summer, laid up to dry and cure. Much of the wood was down wood. Down wood was composed of trees and branches that were knocked down in storms. Last year's wood, cured and dry, would provide the best heat.

Families that had to rely on fireplaces had most of their heat go up the chimneys. Betty and I visited a National Park one winter. They had big stone seats on either side of the walk-in fireplace area. We hated to leave and walk through a foot of snow to our cabin accommodations. But everything you do there is fun, even wading in the snow, dodging buffalos, watching bubbling springs. It was the sweet smell of burning wood in the air that told us some family had their Warm Morning stove stoked with well-cured last fall's cut logs.

We knew their house was toasty; the thin trickle of smoke coming out of the chimney gave it away. No doubt: Pennsylvania or West Virginia anthracite burns in a Base Burner stove.

But the odor that permeated Saint Paul this cold morning was from the least expensive coal available, Sulphur-laden Brazil Indiana lump coal, delivered daily five or six days a week by Harold Scripture and his helper, my oldest brother Leon.

The man from whom Dad bought anthracite coal had a very simple name and for the life of me I can't remember what it was. He owned the string of Grain Elevators alongside the big four-track between Cincinnati and beyond to a large grain terminal in Indianapolis, which is where he had a coal yard. And that's where Dad bought the coal.

BALL LIGHTNING

Mom, Dad and I were sitting on the front porch swinging back and forth, staring at the ominous yellowish sky. Mom thought we should be going into the house before the pending storm hit St. Paul. "A real toad strangler," Dad had predicted with his weather phrasal. It was uncommonly hot; a cool breeze was playing tic-tac-toe on the limber branches in the maple trees. We had the doors open to give us a cooling breeze through the house from the latch-fastened open front door to the open back door.

We were seated in a semi-straight line from the open front door to the open back door. It was a phenomenal sight, never to be repeated in my lifetime. No sooner had we sat down in the living room, toward the front of the house, than the exposition began. There was a hissing noise that moved through the house like a quickly-moving spark of a lengthy lit fuse. It had shape and color. The balls were greenish with red sparkles of light within its straight path of movement, probably an inch in diameter and a foot or so off of the floor. The ball lightning lasted for the entire trip through the house – in the front door, out the back. Then it was gone forever. We all sat there in something of a daze, not understanding what we had just witnessed. Dad called it ball lightning.

"That's something you'll probably *never* see again," Dad said, rather confidently. He was right.

THE BANK FAILURE

It was a very busy well-run prosperous enterprise, the St. Paul Farmer's Bank. Dad was one of the trustees. James told me Dad had all his money deposited in the St. Paul Bank, $20,000, in those days a sizeable amount, when the 1929 crash hit. The sad part, Dad watched his money as it walked out the doors with people who contributed to the demise of the town's former solvent asset, the bank, by drawing out their own accounts. St. Paul never regained its bank until the end of WWII and the boys came home. The smart solvent Waldron Bank bought a Shelby County lot in St. Paul and built a Waldron Branch near the heart of St. Paul, safe and secure in Shelby County.

On our way home from our honeymoon, I stopped at the Waldron Bank, before the Branch, to introduce my wife. Dad was not stingy, just not observant. Mom never had a penny to her name unless she asked for it. I don't think she ever wrote a check or made a deposit. The money in our account was what Betty and I could write checks against. Betty paid the bills and kept the books. Whatever we had was not mine. It was ours!

BEEF BACKBONES

I doubt that you will ever be able to buy meaty beef backbones unless you know someone who raises beef cattle and slaughters it for their own consumption. Then again, the backbone might be too dear to them to sell, it would be to me! But I don't raise young beef.

There is nothing like beef backbones roasted down to an enormously good taste with chips of crust from the roasted meat, almost like a beef cracklin. I know they don't compare to real cracklins but boy, aren't those tastes hard to beat. Thing is, I wonder if I ever will again taste cracklins. I don't mean those sacks of whatever is that they call cracklings. In the old days a real farmer would have been embarrassed to call whatever that stuff is cracklins. Every once in a while I succumb to the cracklings hype. Henry, my cat, is actually smarter than me. Whatever that stuff is, he won't even taste it, let alone eat it.

MY FIRST AIRPLANE RIDE IN 1928

It was a World War I two-place biplane surveying St. Paul, Indiana, with several circling sweeps before flying down the county line road paralleling Platt's farm field, where the barnstormers landed. The mechanic had corralled, with free rides, two strongsters to go to Brunner's filling station to fill and bring back two cans of gasoline. A landing airplane was Lorelei's cry to the adventuresome.

The mechanic had a set of scales on a tripod, a round dial, a round dial on the top, one cent per pound. The pilot was resplendent in knee-length jodhpurs, wool fleece jacket with a fluffed fur collar, brown leather knees-to-ankles leggings laced tight, matching helmet with goggles resting on top at the ready and an extra-long white silk scarf. I had always thought they wore the long scarves to impress the pretty girls. That, too, but really they wore them of silk and extra-long to wrap around their necks so that they would not chafe their necks, turning, twisting, swiveling their heads when looking for enemy planes in a dogfight. Now you know, Snoopy.

Evelyn and Marian alternated care for their five-year-old brother, giving their mother a day off on Saturday. Ev had just graduated from high school. She, her little brother, and a classmate walked out to look at the airplane.

"Do you want to ride in the airplane?" her school friend asked. Ev pointed to me. Having heard the exchange, the pilot reassured her. "Your little brother will be perfectly safe with me," he said. "I can take you all, but I will need a written consent from the boy's mother." I nearly dragged my feet going home. I just knew Mom would say no.

Guess what, Mom signed the consent! I remember everything I saw, and especially my mother standing in the front yard. The kicker: I cost Ev's friend 50 cents. Who knows, the pilot may have been hauling air mail on Monday. He may have been waiting for his commission. He sure got my vote. I bet he liked hauling little boys, too.

I was sitting in the front cockpit in the middle seat between Ev on my left, and her classmate on the right. The mechanic fitted heavy straps around each of us with one strap across the three of us, just to make sure we would all stay in our seats. I was wearing my Christmas present, a black oilcloth helmet with isinglass goggles.

"I'm counting on you to not move around or stand up," said the mechanic, "because all these belts will keep you right here so you will be safe." And he winked at me. Then the mechanic stepped in front of the plane. He twirled the big wooden prop a few times until it seemed to catch.

Then came the back and forth exchange between the pilot and the mechanic.

"Switch on."
"Switch on."
"Contact."
"Contact."

The big Liberty engine roared to life. The pilot signaled. The mechanic pulled out the chocks and we were rolling down the grass strip. The plane lifted as we cleared the fence.

Look, there's the school and gym, 'n' the cemetery, the falls, Flat Rock River. There's Dad's store and Mom in the front yard waving. I would never have been able to see her from that vantage point if she hadn't signed that consent.

BLASTS AT THE RIVER

During the Great Depression, way late after midnight, we would hear a dull boom down towards Flat Rock River. Someone had tossed a lighted stick of dynamite in the river for the fish that it would kill. The dynamiters would gather as many of the big dead fish as they could and scurry, like the nuts they were, away from the river as quickly as they could from Game Wardens. Even so, for days after we would find dead fish and turtles of all species along the bank. So sad.

THE BLOCKHOUSE

In 1930, I don't think anyone ever actually understood why the KKK came down to a level place on the banks of the Flat Rock River between Saint Paul, Saint Omar and Moscow, IN. to build a poured concrete block house with gun ports on all four sides. It sported NO TRESPASSING SIGNS, too. Even after the KKK went kerplunk or belly-up, I don't think many people had the intestinal fortitude to walk up to a porthole and look in. We bike-riding kids did no peeking either. I've been down that road several times and I still haven't looked in.

CAMP ATTERBURY

The Interurban Line was hit the worst. The War in Europe was heating up. Camp Atterbury was under construction to train soldiers.

If the Indianapolis-Cincinnati Interurban Line could have hung on for a few more months, they would have had to put on extra cars to handle the traffic.

Prime Indiana farmland was gobbled up for the construction of Camp Atterbury. Some of the land absorbed had been given to the Revolutionary War soldiers and their land grants had passed down to dirt farmer descendants. I saw several teary-eyed land owners stripped of their property.

The War Department decided to buy land in Indiana for a new state-of-the-art training facility. It wasn't long before we were hearing field artillery and the shouts of men training there. It changed the course of many lives.

THE CAST-IRON HORSE AND MOM'S BIG TOE

I don't know what one of those iron horse weights weighed, but I didn't blame the horses for not moving around too much when their head was fastened to one. Most people used them to insure old dobbin would still be where he or she had been left. Some bribed dobbin with a bag of cracked corn or oats. Oats and rolled oats had the reputation of being too gassy, which was the truth. Just sit next to the driver in a sleigh, buggy or spring wagon. I think that was the reason Mr. Blackamore had a see-through windbreak on his buggy.

On the back porch, the door to the cellar was a heavy slab door covering the stairs down into the basement, counterbalanced with a cast-iron horse weight suspended above the floor on a sash cord running through a pulley attached to the wood ceiling. Mom had trouble with her feet, with bunions the size of hulled walnuts. She walked in bare feet when in the house. We all lifted the cellar door high enough for the counterweight to pull the door open. One day Mom lifted the door and unexpectedly the rope broke. The counterweight slammed into the heavy wood floor, breaking the glass in the windows. The door dropped, cutting off the tip of Mom's right big toe. She hunted around down in the basement to find the severed toe piece. She doused a strip of fat bacon with homeopathic "medicinal turbine," cleaned and fitted the toe piece back on her big toe, draped the bacon over the end of her damaged toe and bandaged it into place. In about a week the toe started itching, a sign of healing. Two days later Mom removed the dressing. The cut-off toe was pink and healthy and perfectly reattached, upside-down! "Grandma, why is that big toe different from the others?" Doris's little kids were fascinated with sight-and-see injuries.

CIDER AND CIDER VINEGAR

We had an old-fashioned yellow sweet apple tree behind the garage. I picked all the apples on the tree and hauled them down the street to a cider press on a "halvers" deal Dad made with the press man. (A "halvers" deal meant the two parties would split the profit.) Two twenty-gallon crocks were sitting in six inches of ice-cold water on the floor in the cellar. Mom had me put our share of the cider into the crocks. Think hot buttered popcorn and ice cold cider. How about hot cider with a cinnamon stick?

POTATOE TIME

We never raised potatoes in the garden. Potatoes took up too much space and were cheap to buy. Oh, once in a while Mom might tear up the spring vegetables and plant a few hills of potatoes. A plate of late green beans cooked with new potatoes was mighty tasty. It's called fingering. With your fingers, you dig into the side of the potato hill and feel for little potatoes. Left alone, in a few weeks they would be big. When Betty and I gardened I always raised potatoes just for the pleasure of digging them up. The potato hills revealed bakers, some fist-size, right on down to golf balls and marbles. I never let Jim and Carolyn dig the potatoes, although they wanted to do so until one forkful under a hill revealed the job was drudgery to everyone except me.

CIVIL WAR VETS

I wasn't very old at the time, perhaps four or five. I started school when I was six. I knew two Civil War veterans, Joe and Ed Eck. They were stone masons and some of the tools of their trade were leaning against their garden fence along the front road parallel to the New York Central railroad tracks. There were two public bridges over Flat Rock River leading into St. Paul. The lower bridge is the iron bridge, now gone, and the other bridge was a beautiful limestone arch, also replaced with a new modern bridge upstream, about a guesstimate half mile and downstream from the NYC railroad bridge a few hundred yards. I don't know whether the Eck brothers had a contract to build the bridge or to furnish the dressed stone from their stone quarry, which was almost within spitting distance of the bridge. If I remember correctly, the bridge had five arches. The Great Depression, at whatever point the quarries were at that moment, put the quarries out of business forever. I can remember an arch on the south side of the river for a spur railroad line running from Greeley's Stone Crusher, through building stone quarries, and on out to the holding sidings alongside the main NYC line.

As teenagers, we boys swam in Greeley's quarry pond. That pond covered seven and a half acres. The derrick timbers were at the southwest corner near where the crusher had been. If we circled the perimeter of the pond we always took at least two of the derrick timbers with us. There was a matching arch on the town side. My memory tells me there were two larger arches for the river. I can almost remember in a big flood when the water went down, the river was going through a different arch. As many times as I walked over and under that bridge, I can't remember that.

SHINNY

In the winter, we ice-skated on Eck's pond. It had silted up from all the floods. At the most it wasn't much deeper than 8 to 12 inches. Our version of ice hockey was shinny. The shinny sticks came from the profusion of sandbar willows that grew in clumps around the edges of the pond. You found a skinny tree with a slight curve at the bottom. The puck was a no. 2½ tin peach can salvaged from the dump and flattened. There were several hazards playing shinny. You had to dodge the grass clump that stuck up above the ice. You stood a chance of getting checked into a stand of willows. There probably was only one good pair of ice skates in the whole bunch.

Bill was the veterinarian's son. Doc had a brother living in Colorado. Bill had real shoe skates, he had real skis, but that's another story and more than likely he had a real hockey stick and a real puck, but some of that stuff you can't flash in front of just anybody. My ice skates were the clamp-on type. Likely they were in the attic when Dad bought that big house with indoor plumbing that didn't work very well until after WWII, when the town was ordered to put in a sewer system and city water for the 750 inhabitants of St. Paul.

CLARA AND CATHERINE

After school let out in April, farm kids were needed to work on the farms, so my cousin Mary Lois spent two weeks down on the farm visiting her country cousins Clara and Catherine back home in Johnson County. They were the only two to whom Mary could confide her deplorable home life conditions. They were the only friends who could offer solace without repercussions. Can you imagine two weeks of pleasure, while waiting at home was Simon Legree?

COKE MACHINE

In those days they called traveling salesmen The Drummers and it seemed like a very profitable vocation from the numbers who stopped at Dad's store businesses. One particular fellow I remember was driving a brown-colored business vehicle and he hopped out with a black drummer's case in hand. Cars only came in three colors; black, brownish, and purple. "Mr. Nail," he said to Roe Whiteinger, a clerk. "No, that is Mr. Nail standing back there with the boy, his son."

"Mr. Nail, I have something in this case that will help you boost your sales. Something your son has probably tasted, Coca Cola? Coca Cola sells very well, and I like NEHI grape, orange and root beer."

"No," Dad said, "I couldn't sell Coca Cola; the restaurant sells Coca Cola and I will not get into competition with them, they need those sales."

Dad, a merchant with integrity, passed up many such potential lucrative sales. Eventually Dad had to succumb to our competition, Barley, the drug store, and yes, the restaurant.

CHRISTMAS CANDY

Dad's Christmas candy tradition will always be one of my fondest memories from working at his store. Each December Dad made a trip to Indianapolis to get a supply of candy for Christmas gift bags. While I have a vague memory of what the candy store owner looked like, I don't recall the name of the store.

Each bag that was prepared for the children who came in the store contained a variety of hard candy, probably six or so different types. He used the brown paper sacks that looked like small lunch bags, perhaps six inches high. I remember candy varieties that ran the gamut, from the ribbon candy that came in long thin pieces to the 'rock' candy that had a color around the edge, white inside – with a swirl of color in the very center. Some of the candy had a tasty peanut butter flavor. And the jewel of each package was a chocolate drop, which was about an inch and a half in diameter and equally tall. The inside was white, wonderfully flavored, covered with rich chocolate.

I accompanied Dad more than once when he made the Indianapolis candy run. Gathering the store personnel around him, the proprietor would say, "Now this is the way to sell candy." I think the point of that comment was twofold. First, he wanted to encourage his personnel to strive for volume sales; second, he wanted to publicly acknowledge Dad for his generous purchase. While I don't remember the exact amount, I recall thinking that Dad was spending a considerable amount of money on this complementary candy endeavor. When I inquired as to why he would spend so much on the candy, Dad's response was typically modest. "Well, it's something that our customers really appreciate." I always thought it was also something Dad believed to be the right thing to do, given that he was among the most successful business men in the community.

To show the depth of his appreciation, the candy dealer would give Dad a box of his finest chocolates. "These are for the wife," he would say. Dad appreciated that, as did Mother, of course. We (the children) would usually get to sample a piece or two, and I recall that the chocolates were delicious.

The daughters of the proprietor would pull Dad aside on his way out to emphasize the family's gratitude. "Mr. Nail," the one daughter would say, "we want to express our sincere appreciation for your purchase. You're, without a doubt, one of our best customers."

One interesting aspect of the Christmas candy tradition was the number of non-customers that would show up expecting candy for their children. Dad's intention was to provide the candy for the children of his regular customers. Once the word got out, however, strangers would appear in the store inquiring about the candy. Dad would have been justified had he turned them away with an explanation. But he never did. Any family that entered the premises with children left with a bag of candy. The wonderful thing, of course, is that Dad's generosity resulted in the joy and happiness of many children, which was especially nice a Christmas time.

COME CLIMB ME

We were walking along the old right of way going towards St. Paul. For some reason wild strawberries grew there. Being perpetually hungry boys even though Mrs. Townsend outdid herself for dinner, we stopped to pick a handful upon which to munch. We had the bluff of the hill overlooking Flat Rock Run and the stone abutments still standing in place, those that had carried the bridge across the river.

A sandbar willow that had grown up next to an abutment appealed to us, crying out, "Come climb me, come up on top of the abutment." A siren's call not to be ignored. John, being the oldest and strongest, started up the tree with Dick right behind him. John was just feet away from the top of the abutment when he shouted, "Go back, Dick. I can't make it."

"I can't, John, try harder."

"I'm slipping; you'll have to go back, Dick."

I was still on the ground cradling my single-shot BB gun. Suddenly, it was up to me to break this stalemate. I slipped a BB into the muzzle of my gun. I could hear the BB rolling down the barrel. I cocked the gun, brought it up to my shoulder, took careful aim and shot John in the derriere. It was all the impetus John needed to reach the top. Dick was up there quick as a squirrel. Guess he didn't want or need a BB.

When I got up on the top, John didn't even thank me for my help. Of course he may have still been smarting!

DAD'S GOODIES

Every one of the Nail children, including myself, could tell you what was in Dad's sack of food goodies that he took for the fishing buddies. For a good long time, it was Dad and Berry Copeland until Jim wouldn't let his dad drive anymore, then it was Dad, Berry and Louis (Chick) Leffler, with James H. Naile doing the driving.

DAD'S MEDICINE

Mom, and later, our beloved stepmother Aunt Sadie, would measure out two tablespoons of bourbon to stir into an earthenware cup with squeezed lemon juice, a teaspoon of sugar, and filled the rest of the way with hot water, to make a bedtime hot toddy for our perpetually chilled Father.

Isn't it strange, that bottle of whisky set there on the pantry shelf within easy reach, but it was not a temptation for anyone in the family, and no one else in the family ever tasted it simply because it was Dad's bedtime warming medicine.

In the winter, Dad wore one-piece wool union suits under his outer clothing. Even with that, he was cold.

In the summer he wore two-piece cotton BVDs. The sleeves ended just above his elbow, the trousers just below his knee. The top piece was buttoned to the trousers. Dad would have been at a loss with boxers or jockeys. I can't see Dad in a sleeveless undershirt or a t-shirt.

Year-round, Dad wore starched collars fastened to collarless white shirts with a brass fastener in the back of the collar shirt band to keep the two pieces together. Dad sent the collars to Indianapolis to be re-starched. It was a sad day when Dad had to give up his stiff collars and wear white Arrow shirts.

THE DARK AGES

I didn't recognize their voices. Someone coughed and said, "Remember that other one we strung up here, and now we got these two they kicked off that freight train, just a little while ago. You gonna help us? Should be easy, whatever time you want to do it."

Only one person was talking. I heard the story repeated several times but I never heard their names. Men like these never want to be identified or have their deeds revealed. Glad I never knew who they were and never heard any names.

The trees on that corner were eventually cut down. Good riddance. I don't know for sure, but someone might have replaced the trees with a big boulder.

THE DEMISE OF THE STONE ARCH BRIDGE

I suppose it was inevitable. I don't remember the year, but Flat Rock was so low, the far end of the bridge Arch began to sag. Seems like money to level the sag was sparse and the fix turned out to be loads of crushed stone fortified with hot tar dumped into the swag. It was sort of like a band aid on a broken arm. The popular prognostication was that the far end of the bridge was built on a rediscovered mud seam, which is not uncommon in rivers with stone bottoms. Generally the best repair is to drive full tree-length hardwood logs into the mud seam. As long as the logs are covered with water the bridge will function strong and sturdy.

> *Note: An old bridge in the southern part of Indiana was slated for replacement. When the bridge was dismantled, the original oak log pilings were found in the mud seams. The logs pulled up out of the seams were sent to a mill to be reclaimed. They proved to be in excellent condition and have been milled for recycling. This story is circa 1920.*

FAMILY NUANCE

We'd been waiting patiently, the wives chagrined at the extra hours we were there. We were reassured: you wait for good customers. These good families would be at a country church in the morning, after the early morning chores, milking the cows, mucking out the stalls, feeding the horses. Bone-tired for sure. Some of the men would receive a sharp elbow during the sermon. There'd be sheepish looks.

The coal oil tank was locked when Norman went home. We'd swept the store. The lights were winked out, the back door barred, the front door key locked, and we'd walk around the corner and head for home. Then we could smell it as we walked up the front steps onto the porch. The pan was 9x12x2½ inches. We never knew what fruit would be on hand to inspire Mom any Saturday evening, but it would be one of her fabulous applesauce, cherries, peaches, apricots, raisins, apples or whatever was available for spice cake loaded with the featured combination of fruit, still warm from the oven, with ice-cold milk for Dad and James, water for me.

From Mom I had inherited the Burgett curse, a phobia against milk, buttermilk, cold butter, whipped cream, and cream in coffee. I could eat butter melted on toast, biscuits, cornbread, popcorn, and baked potatoes. Dad said of Uncle Will that if Will passed the butter dish, he scrubbed his hands on his table napkin. Most farmer Burgetts separated the cream from the milk and churned the butter and buttermilk for sale. They ate cheese; but they did not drink milk, eat butter, cook with butter or eat mashed potatoes with butter in them. You get the idea?

FLAT ROCK RIVER

Flat Rock River is a well-named river. The majority of the river bed is water-worn flat limestone. I have waded in several sections of it. In other sections, the river is rather foreboding, and even thinking about going into the water would make me uneasy. There are lots of potholes, some swimmable, others like the whirlpool hole that you avoid. The story is there is a down-slope drop in the river where the water picks up speed. When it hits the bottom of the slope, it curls back upon itself, causing the whirlpool that some unknowing stranger got sucked into and drowned. Looking at the pothole, you cannot see this whirlpool action. And I never ever wanted to test it to see if what they said was true. I never knew who "they" were either.

Dad had picked a prime spot to do some serious fishing. I was fishing a pot hole upstream no way close to the whirlpool and Aunt Sadie and Betty were thrashing the water where they were fishing, and talking, both no-no's to dedicated fishermen, and they were catching sun fish, their stringer loaded with pan fish. Dad had started at a spot about 20 feet below the girls. Dad kept inching closer until he was right in between and of course, the fish knew a professional was in the midst and they quit biting. Rather uncanny, don't you think?

THE FOUNDLING

Rod and Maybell loved children. They had planned for a family but it just seemed they were never to be so blessed.

Rod was a successful farmer, even though his spread was small in comparison to those who had nearly sixty cleared acres. As with most farmers in that day, they were self-sufficient, did not owe the bank, went to a little struggling church, and paid their tithe every Sunday. Rod was from the old school. He would continue clearing his fields.

Maybell was the perfect housewife. She was an adept seamstress. She sewed most of the clothing she and Rod wore, including their Sunday best, which she kept hanging on special pegs in the closet in their well-built cabin. She had even managed to make bib overalls for her man.

Rod pulled his heavy coat collar up around his ears to ward off the morning chill. He picked up the two scrubbed clean milk buckets, the larger bucket for the Holstein, the smaller pail for the pampered Jersey. She did not produce as much milk as her bigger mate, but her milk was butter-fat rich. Rod stepped out the door. There was a tightly woven hickory slat egg basket setting on the small porch. Rod set the buckets down, picked up the basket. He opened the door. "Mother, come quick."

The baby was wrapped in a small, tattered, almost threadbare quilt encasing his little body. He was a cheerful little fellow. An upturned toothless grin creased his diminutive mouth. There was a nearly empty thick glass baby bottle with a well-used off-color nipple in the corner of the basket. The boy was wearing a lightweight, fine-knit white undershirt, a tricorn garnet held together with a safety pin, close-knit blue soft fluff wool hose, gloves, slippers and over it all, a blue Canton flannel shift.

Maybell and Rod were flabbergasted. They did not know of any expectant mothers. Neither did the neighbors or the Sheriff who inquired about it in a wider neighborhood. In the end the baby remained with Maybell and Rod.

"What shall we name our son?"

Rod opened the door. Streaks of light announced the borning of a new day. The pinpoints of stars that had blanketed the sky, winked out. In the distance, a small bright cluster.

Pointing, Rod said, "There is our son's name! Morning Star."

Hopefully, a bereaved mother would know her little boy was safe, in a real home, with loving parents.

> *NOTE: Dad said Morning Star was well known in the area and was a great help to his parents. He was a beloved only son. His birth mother was never found or identified, and no one ever claimed to know who she could be.*

FRANK, THE ICE MAN

> *NOTE: I can't remember her given name. For this incident Frank's wife will be called "MARN."*

Frank and Jen were brother and sister. They frequently chatted when Jen passed by Frank's home on her way uptown. Frank and Marn lived in a house attached to Frankie's flat metal business storefront at the edge of the business district. Frank was a tinsmith. He installed metal roofs, shaped and installed gutters, downspouts, cupolas, vents, other metal objects, tarred and re-tarred semi-flat metal roofs. In the summer Frank delivered ice. To keep dry, he wore a long leather apron on his back. Customers would put a card showing the amount of ice they wanted in a window facing the road. Frank would chip off that amount from bug-scored blocks of ice on his truck. Kids would follow the ice truck and Frank always managed to find ice pieces to hand out. Grimy little hands turned cleaned as youngsters cradled, licked, sucked and munched those special treats. I can remember eating spalls of ice from the back of Frankie's truck. Frank stored the ice in a heavily insulated room, about 18 inches of sawdust between tongue and groove 2-by-6 timbers built in a large shed behind his shop. Ice was kept up into summer before commercial ice was available, and many farmers stored ice in this fashion. Frank caught, dressed and sold turtle meat. They don't call them snapping turtles for no reason.

FREE NYC TRAIN RIDE? SURE!

Vagrant: a person who wanders from place to place, shiftless, jobless, supporting himself by begging; Hobo: a migrating worker, wanderer, tramp. They were men, both young and old, hobo-ing in the terrible great depression, a happening not of their choosing. I have read that hoboes that got a good meal marked the premises in a secret way, so that future hoboes would know to stop there. Usually the hoboes that came to Mom's back door seemed to know in advance there would be hot coffee, a wholesome sandwich, sometimes bread and gravy, a piece of pie, cake or a cookie. I can remember Mom frying eggs for hot sandwiches. Mom had rules and boundaries, but sometimes these vagabonds went away with an apple in their pocket. Many were war veterans.

We did not see many hoboes in St. Paul because they rode the freight trains and freight trains seldom stopped in St. Paul unless they were shunted off on a siding because of higher-priority, through trains. The few we did see were usually the hoboes that the New York Central security had kicked off a waiting freight train. A fifteen-mile walk to the county seat would take them where they had a better chance to hop another freight train. In a display of cruelty to the down-trodden, they were a big laugh for the guys that had good paying railroad jobs. So what if the fellows they left out in the sticks were veterans? Just doing my job!

GREELEY'S POND

As I mentioned earlier, we often swam in the 7½ acre Greeley Pond. The limestone mined in this quarry was sold as crushed stone. The derrick timber floated on the bank where the crusher was located. We took derrick timbers with us and swam around the perimeter of the pond. Flat Rock River in flood stage flowed into this pond. It was well stocked with pan fish, bass, freshwater jelly fish and probably catfish.

HENRY AND HENRY

If there was a reason, I don't remember what it was, but it seemed all my sisters and brothers were present and we were telling funny stories about each other or ourselves. This one was a winter incident involving Henry the Milkman leaving two quarts of milk and Doris' Tom cat, Henry. I don't know what kind of mischievousness Henry Cat had got into but whatever it was, he was on the fly out the back door with my sister Doris' broom upraised, hot on his trail and yelling, "Get out of here, Henry." Henry the Cat wasn't confused, but Henry Corey, the Milkman, was at seeing the menacing broom circling around above his head. He dropped the two quarts of milk and made a beeline towards his truck. Henry the Cat's little pink tongue was lapping up the spill. Watch out for the broken glass, Henry. Rosie (born Jan. 15, 1930) cried as if Henry the Cat understood every word. I think he must have because Henry the Cat avoided the twirling broom and slivers of glass as he escaped under the lilac bush that had dropped all its foliage in the fall.

HOMEMADE

It was one of those family reunion get-togethers, sharing a big meal. A meal would not be a meal if Mom's big pot of chicken and dumplings weren't on the table or platters of fried chicken, with gravy made with small pieces of skillet scrapings, converted with milk and flour into a tasty gravy blanket for mashed potatoes or little torn pieces of bread, a time-tested family treat.

Little kids, on the run, were screeching at brother, sister, cousin. A hot afternoon, Mom on a trip to the basement, reappeared with two quarts of her home bottled purple grape juice, ice cold from sitting in about two and a half inches of welling-up spring water. Mom opened the second jar and carried it around for refills. Bob Steiner held out his glass, crying out, ready, ready! He took a drink and proclaimed, "That is the best sweet wine I have had in ages." Mom took the glass from Bob's hand and emptied the liquid in a flower bed then she upended the canning jar and emptied it, too.

"Oh, Mary Alice, why did you do that?"

Right then, Bob learned, our mother was the Carry Nation of our family.

THE HONEY DIPPER

Every spring, he was a much-needed independent businessman coming into St. Paul and other small towns dotting Indiana. He was driving the same spavined horses, a horse disease where deposits of bone form or lymph, a yellowish fluid that forms in joints, usually causing lameness to his team of horses.

His team was pulling a large forum wagon containing six steel barrels and an array of dipper shovels and two sacks of lime, a natural cleansing material. His job was to clean the conveniences behind each home that were positioned parallel to the alley, dumping the waste in barrels. The disposition of the travel contents was up to the honey dipper; defiantly not in the river or a farm field, unless the farmer wasn't home. Free fertilization, don't you know. I didn't know how the honey dipper was paid, whether by each family or by the town. All I can say is be careful where you step. Riders on trains weren't supposed to flush the toilets in town, so it was not uncommon to see toilet paper stuck to the cross ties after fast passenger trains barreled through St. Paul. "Oh, was that a town? Yes, I'll watch it, uh huh, I'll be careful, uh huh!"

One year they dropped our convenience and tore off the roof.

When the Honey Dippers were in town, out along the interurban tracks was a choice space to dump the barrels of waste. You had to be careful where you walked. And of course, you had to exercise the same care after those passenger trains had traveled through and beyond St. Paul in either direction. A lot of people called the conveniences by their common two-word vernacular.

INDIANA'S HOMEGROWN KKK

The following incident, Indiana politics, happened in the really dark ages of the History of the State of Indiana. The Indianapolis Mayor and the Indiana Governor thought they were so powerful they could do as they pleased with impunity, without the need of recourse. This high-handedness culminated in the rape and murder of a very pretty young school teacher in a private railroad car en route to Chicago in 1928. The Governor, D.C. Stephenson, was indicted, convicted, and served time for murder. After several years of imprisonment, sick and dying, he was paroled and allowed to return to his native Tennessee. The preceding is a brief and likely inaccurate synopsis. Several books have been written about the case. Worth reading.

THE INDIANAPOLIS MOBILE LETTER

The right of way. In those days practically all passenger trains except locals like old jerk had railway post offices with a crew of railway postal clerks working mail. St. Paul often got first class mail delivered on the fly from these trains. In front of the St. Paul post office was a crank out and up to an open-door-height frame upon which a special pouch for first class mail could be hung. There was an elbow arm on the train's mail car that the clerk extended to catch the mail pouches. The St. Paul delivery point for first class mail and newspapers was at a designated drop point where County Line Road intersected the train tracks. Once in a while the newspapers got sucked under the train and cut up because some person or vehicle was waiting too close to the tracks in the delivery area. The post office clerk only had a few seconds to decide where to kick off the mail pouch and newspaper sacks. I can remember walking the tracks along with other scavengers trying to find enough newspaper for Dad to read—and the funnies, too.

JEN AND HER DOG, JACK

Jen and Jack walked uptown to get the mail, visit and shop. Jack was territorial. He did not take his responsibilities lightly. It was Jack's duty to assure their rite of passage was identified and safe. Trees, shrubs, bushes and lilacs lined the route, each to be inspected to receive Jack's seal of approval. Jack had long since inspected Frank's front screen door and added it to his itinerary. In the pre air-conditioned summers, people opened doors and windows to catch stray breezes.

Marn smelled a pungent odor wafting through the house. No use asking Frank about it for he had long since burned out his olfactory faculties with the hot materials of his trade. One morning, Marn caught Jack adding his seal of approval to the screen door. Spraying the screen door with turpentine, Clorox then ammonia only encouraged Jack to redouble his efforts to overcome the unknown rival. Imagine the dialogue between Frank, Marn and finally Jen. Looking for a tool in the shop, Frank found a serviceable lamp cord. Baring the wire, he wove the cord into the screen door. Early the next morning, when Frank unplugged the cord, Jack was frozen in his ceremonial stance. At long last, bone-dry, his set of suspended toenails joined their other three companion sets of suspended toe nails and with anguished wails, mimicking St. Paul's fire engine siren, Jack ran for home, shaken.

The next morning Jack was back on his inspection route applying his seals of approval. When he and Jen got to that place, Jack carefully stepped off the sidewalk and took a circuitous path to avoid his unknown adversary.

THE KKK STRIKES OUT

The uniformed contingent got out of a large black automobile. Two of the men went to the back of the sedan, opened the trunk and took out a large thin cardboard box and followed the other four into the store. The box bearers opened the box, extracted a large white metal sign. They positioned the sign to face Dad so he could read the inscription. I recall such a white sign down near Barley's cash register; I remember knowing the inscription.

Dad never was a very big man. I doubt if he weighed as much as 145 pounds. These brave visitors should not have labored under the assumption that intimidation was going to cow this merchant. The sign contained the usual vitriolic language of the hate group. As they had succeeded doing with their overwhelming tactics in so many other businesses, they now declared to Dad, "We are going to hang this sign, 'THIS IS A KKK STORE,' in a prominent place in this store."

So that there would be no misunderstanding, addressing the obvious leader of this pack, Dad's admonishment was delivered in his normal speaking voice, "No, you are not!"

They all looked bewildered in their ankle-length bed-sheet garb with their eyes and mouth openings in their peaked headpieces. Since they thought they held the heavy hand, they were aghast at Dad's rebuke. They milled about trying to regroup.

"We'll put you out of business."

Then there was that pesky string bean again, in that normal speaking voice, "Go ahead if you think you can."

I never asked Dad if he knew any of his assailants. Had he, he would not have told me, particularly if they were from St. Paul or local environs.

LA BOCA GRANDE

Westbrook Peggler was *The Indianapolis Star* Political Columnist. Peggler hated President Roosevelt's wife Eleanor with a passion. I think it was for all she was trying to do for the downtrodden, hence La Boca Grande—humongous Big Talking Mouth. Westbrook never wrote a column in which he didn't lambaste her in the most unflattering ways, mocking La Boca Grande, Eleanor.

Of course there were, like it is now, the native rabble agreeing with every word and there were the opposing side putting in their two cents' worth on a scant ratio of not quite 50-50; that kept the pot boiling and warm.

Dad did not like Westbrook, and yet he had to read his column every day to find out what was riling Peggler.

One thing about Dad, he never discussed politics, religion, or gossip about local people, anything that could be controversial. Neither would he answer negative questions.

I liked Dad's style and adopted it myself when I was on my own. You'd be amazed at what a properly used smile will disarm!

LEM AND YELLER

Eccentric Lem (his real name I don't recall), the farmer? Of course he was. Lem's main farming companion was his horse, Ole Yeller. There was a steady stream of talk between Lem and Ole Yeller with Lem doing most of the conversing for both of them, and Ole Yeller rolling his eyes and cropping off all the green grass he could stretch and strain his scrawny neck to reach.

Dad happened by Lem's cornfield when Lem and Yeller were cultivating the corn. Dad had noticed that the stalks in the ends of several rows were mashed flat. Lem had hold of his old horse's blinders. Lem pulled Yeller's head down so that they were just about eyeball to eyeball. "Now Yeller, look at that row. You mashed the stalks almost flat again. You just won't pay no 'tenshun to what I'm a'tellin' yah. Now I want yah to pay close 'tenshun. I'm going to show yah whatcher doin' wrong." Then Lem stood in front of the horse and the corn and he proceeded to stomp down the rest of the row of corn. "Yeller, if yah'd just walk to the end of the row and out into the fence row aways an' turn 'round, that would be capital and the corn would be aw'right. Giddy-up, Yeller," . . . as Lem reined Ole Yeller into position to smash down the few still standing stalks at the end of another row.

"Yeller, know what yah jist did? I'm gonna show yah."

MATILDA BURNS

Concerning Matilda Burns, conjecture: It was not uncommon in that day for a good-hearted man to marry a young woman with child so that the child would be born with a reliable surname. The actual father of Matilda's child was a scoundrel who ducked out on his responsibility.

I think Dad would have been the kind of responsible young man who would have seen in Matilda a good young lady in a precarious situation, and he would not have wanted to see her and her child's name dragged through the mud. Fortunately, we will never know!

MOM'S CHRISTMAS TREE

The six-foot-tall scrub wild Christmas tree, I had found in a fence row and brought home. Mom had her strings and strings of electric Christmas tree lights and silver icicles that she had painstakingly fashioned from the tin foil that came in the heavy tea boxes placed in them to protect the tea from the elements. Dad bought gun powder, green and black tea in their original heavy wooden chests that originated in the orient, from a wholesale house in Indianapolis. He also bought Dar Jeeling and India teas in their original containers. Rather than tin foil, these teas were packed in paper so transparent that Dad could read his Bible through thick bundles of it. Mom had glass balls that had come from her parents' Christmas tree. Dad developed his own ice tea mixture. It was so popular that he had customers from as far away as Indianapolis, Cincinnati come just for the tea. I watched Dad mix it many times and I had customers willing to buy my rendition of Dad's mixture. It was not as good and I tried to convince everybody that insisted I make a sack of tea that it wasn't as good as Dad's mixture. They would ask if I used the same varieties of tea Dad used. I assured them it was but mine was flawed. Dad's tea tasted better than mine. I guess if you lived in Cincinnati and you kept hearing about the best-ever iced tea mixture, mine would have to suffice, if it were your only choice. Gun Powder is a variety of green tea and it got its name, if I remember correctly, from the way it was rolled by the leaf pickers as they plucked the leaves from the tea bushes.

MOM'S GREENHOUSE

A chipped Ball Mason green glass canning jar was never discarded in the dump; it became a miniature greenhouse sheltering a slip from some pretty rose that would be rooting under that little green canopy. Mom might have as many as a dozen greenhouses at work. Mom's rooting powder was her love of flowers, her TLC. Mom was always generous with flower starts.

MOM'S PAN FISH

All the fish mentioned in the foregoing stories are worth eating if they are on the menu. Unfortunately, you'll never be able to enjoy, served with a big bowl of fluffy mashed potatoes, Mom's pan fish dipped in a little amount of flour mixed with stone ground corn meal, fried in fresh bacon grease, done to a turn. And neither will I ever again.

MR. BLACKAMORE'S SEDAN

If we worked in Dad's store, Dad paid us. At eight or nine, I could deliver groceries in my red coaster wagon, put up groceries on the shelves as high as I could reach, and sweep. Dad never expected more than I was capable of doing.

We had a few customers coming to the store on horseback. They generally brought a gunny sack in which to carry those purchases. There were some that came in brown or natural-color spring wagons and Mr. Blackamore came in his closed, polished black sedan pulled by a span of brushed slick, anthracite black mares, wearing a beaded throw with dangling beaded tassels to ward off the pesky flies. They would tie up at the kitchen rail of a section of log chain strung between three hemlock posts. For some of the horses, chomping was just to ease their boredom. But what if there was no space at the rail?

Mr. Blackamore pulled into the empty lot behind the old bank building. We lifted a 40-pound horse weight out of the luggage box on the back of the sedan and looped the horse's reins through the loop on top of the weight, No way was that mare going to move forty pounds of cast iron looped around its neck. Chomping time was at hand again.

MRS. BRIGHT READS HISTORY

Mrs. Bright was a farm widow. She and her son were still farming the home-place farm. I was a youngster learning the ropes in Dad's store. Mrs. Bright extracted a newspaper clipping she wanted to read to me, from an Indianapolis newspaper. She had been ten years old when she read Lincoln's Gettysburg address, and now at this reading her eyes glistened. When President Lincoln was assassinated her parents took her to see the black bunting-draped train as it passed through Indiana to Illinois.

I thanked Mrs. Bright. I didn't realize it at the time, but I had just witnessed a piece of history.

NOT THE BEE'S KNEES

You could tell a bee tree if a big crowd of bees were massed together, standing on each other and buzzing like a broken guitar with an out of tune string, and entering into a bee tree like it was the first day of Christmas with the bargain crowd, which is about the very best comparison, since the hole into the bee tree was bee size. Like after the sale at midnight, a hole in the bee tree, rendered by some hunter, would be fist size. And if he got stung, it served him right. Sort of 'as is' with the Early Bird Fighters at the Bargain Sales.

Be fair; leave some honey for the Queen and Her Retinue. Remember the Worker bees went into the bee tree toting one tiny sweet bit of honey gathered from the forest's largess one drop at a time, to be deposited in a self-manufactured, master-designed heavy duty wax container.

OLD FUTILITY

Dad chewed tobacco. Once in a while someone would give Dad a cigar. Sometimes Dad would smoke the cigar and I do remember Dad taking a large bite of the cigar to chew it. We sold cheap cigars and really good cigars. There was a cigar manufacturing plant in Terre Haute. Guess what, I was a school-age kid and I could sell any kind of tobacco the customer wanted and I did. That age law hadn't passed yet. Handling tobacco wasn't ever a lure for me. We sold plug tobacco and I cut the size of plug the customers wanted. Plug tobacco that had sweet molasses in the plug. The plug was scored so we could cut the exact size the customer requested. Sometimes Dad would make his own chewing tobacco. There were a few men in town that would grow their own chewing tobacco. Dad would buy fresh tobacco leaf from one of the town growers in order to make his own leaf chewing tobacco. Dad would take the fresh leaves and twist them together. He would hang them in a drying place to cure the tobacco so he would have a fresh twist.

PETS

When I was a youngster growing up, we always had pets. As names go, I don't think we were too original. Seems like we had several dogs named Jack. We called the garage the barn, and that is where Jack slept on an old wool quilt. Jack didn't mind sharing the quilt with Tom, Tommy, Kit and Kitty. I know Kit and Kitty never had kittens. Mom must have given them away because I don't think she had them fixed.

In those days, Ed, an elderly neighbor who apparently did not like pets, would stomp his feet, bark, growl, hiss, run howling towards Jack until Jack had to be sent home with Uncle Govee down on the farm. Then Ed had the audacity to ask one of us kids, "Where is your dog?" Mother would not let us say what we wanted to, "I think he ran away"; instead we had to give a truthful answer.

PINKIE KERR

The men that worked in the quarry kept their dynamite in a small building at the south edge of town. Whenever Pinkie Kerr (I don't recall his actual given name, but everyone called him Pinkie) happened to pass by the storage shed, he would routinely check to see if it happened to be left unlocked. Of course the vast majority of the time it was in fact locked.

I should note that even though he came from a good family, to say that Pinkie was something of a deviant would be a gross understatement.

One day Pinkie got lucky, finding the dynamite shed unlocked as he passed by. The crew was not in the immediate area, but since there was more blasting to do later in the day, the building had been left open.

Pinkie knew if he used a long enough fuse, he could make his way back to town before the blast would erupt. He also knew if he would happen to be with the right person when the explosion occurred, he would have a witness to attest to his innocence. And that's why Pinkie made a point to seek out Aunt Maudie in order to secure his alibi.

Just a minute or so before the overpowering blast rocked the entire St. Paul area, breaking out virtually every window within three to four miles, Pinkie walked up to Aunt Maudie to say hello.

Bless Aunt Maudie's heart, "Well that is *one* thing they can't blame on Pinkie Kerr," Aunt Maudie would repeatedly declare. "He was standing right here talking to me when it blew up."

PSALM 155—THE PIPE

For over 300 years, the Red Stone ceremonial pipe has been prized above all others by the American Indian. Reverence for the place from which it came was common to all Indians and many legends relate the supernatural origin of those quarries and of the first pipe, a gift from the gods. The bowl was the altar; the tobacco, the sacred offering. The smoke carried messages to the gods. Discussions were arranged, treaties solemnized, land acquired, wars begun and terminated, all over a pipe.

Because of the great role the American Indian contributed in shaping the history of the United States, these quarries were set aside as a National Monument to tell part of this story. Today by special law, the historic stone is still reserved for the Indian. Each year a few still quarry the stone to carve ceremonial pipes in the traditional way. I received the above information when I got my pipe. The pipe was meticulously carved by a third-generation pipe maker. The legend of the Four Winds Pipe had been painstaking carved into the bowl by the artisan.

EAST—The sun rises in the east, and brings the beginning of the day.

NORTH—Brings the hardships, the discomfort, and winter's cold winds.

SOUTH—Brings the good things of life, the warm winds of summer, and the growing season.

WEST—The sun sets in the west, and brings the end of the day.

THE QUARRY

The quarry workers built abutments on both sides of the river at Greeley's quarry and downriver at the other quarries. Four steel cables were strung to make wooden-floored swinging foot bridges. In a winter flood, Greeley's Bridge was nearly destroyed. We could walk the cables to get across. I think the lower bridge was still usable. The great depression had shut down a lucrative enterprise and the maintenance of the foot bridges. The business never recovered.

RURALISM

One afternoon Ev and Bob Steiner came home to St. Paul for Mom's fried chicken, hot biscuits, and all the trimmings, including Mom's hand-churned (my job) prized pineapple ice. They arrived early and Bob thought he would gain experience if he could wait on a customer. Dad said, "Sure you can if you want to try it." Just like Columbus, Bob embarked on St. Paul's brand of Ruralism. Dad, Norman and I were busy with other customers.

When Ebb, a rather eccentric dirt farmer from south of St. Paul, strode in, he became Bob's customer. Dad handed Bob a new order pad and a sharpened NO 2 Dixon lead pencil.

"Can I help you?" Bob asked Ebb. Ebb pulled a slip of paper out of his bib overalls, and consulted it.

"Yes, I'll take two rolls of Bung Fodder."

"Beg your pardon?" queried Bob

Taking the pencil, Ebb pointed to the top of the showcase refrigerator where we stacked the toilet paper. We could not afford to waste any space, Ebb's Bung Fodder included.

"Do you have a convenience for a female adolescent?"

Bob was back on the slippery slope. Getting down to the common vernacular, Ebb answered Bob's question—sanitary paper for a young girl.

THE SECRET

Clara Jane's husband, Bill Douglass, saw Norman and Dad coming out of a package store in Shelbyville. Dad was carrying a bottle-shaped brown paper sack. Slyly, Bill was sure he had stumbled onto a closely guarded family secret. "Does Uncle Sherman drink?" he inquired as he triumphantly related the incident. Dad's semi-nightly hot toddy was a pin in Bill's balloon of discovery.

SHERMAN THE LENIENT

I cannot imagine Teacher Dad meting out punishment. At home, Mom was the Simon Legree of punishment. I don't know how it was with my brothers and sisters, but to me, a simple look of disappointment from Mom was a cat-of-nine tails; a sad red eye, the guillotine or being tied to the mast, cut to ribbons with a black snake whip. I can still remember and feel Mom's disappointment.

I remember boyhood friends' talk of punishment "the old man" administered. Whatever age I was at the time, my dad was always fifty-one years older than me. Young friends called their dads the Old Man. I never called my father the Old Man simply because he was not an old man, he was my dad. PERIOD. Hearing a youngster speaking of the old man set Dad's teeth on edge.

SHUCKING CORN

I have seen farmers harvesting corn from the shucks. They used what is called a shucking peg. Dad stocked shucking pegs in the store. Most of the farmers were right-handed and they needed right-handed pegs. Left-handed farmers would tell Dad to order them left-handed pegs. I tried and never could get the hang of using a peg, although it sure did look easy in the hands of the experts. The peg separates ears from the shucks. My memory tells me the peg was about four or five inches long, perhaps ½ inch wide and had a hook bill on both ends; all in a chamois weight leather glove. I guess the two hooks made the peg last longer.

The wagon into which the corn was thrown, on the opposite side of the shuckers, had a fairly tall bunk board to contain the ears. Really good shuckers could make the ears rattle off the bunk board.

You have to hand it to Iowans. They don't want all the old customs to die out. If it isn't Audubon, it's a town in the vicinity where they plant a field of corn so that genuine Iowa farmers can come in with their shucking pegs in the fall, after the last big frost, to turn their clocks back to when!

It would be nice if they had two pair of double thumb cotton shucking gloves sticking out of their hip pockets, too. The above paragraphs are why, in our day, Indiana farm boys were such good basketball players, and if they ever grew up, why they were such good fighters taking on neighboring Waldron's same-age old guys, fighting over the outcome of basketball games, of course!

THE SLED

Everybody wants something special for Christmas that they just know they are not going to get, but figure it doesn't hurt to dream. Billy's uncle in Colorado sent him a flexible flier sled. He could actually steer his flexible flier around big boulders, bushes and trees. I could do it too, by dragging my feet and bouncing my sled just right, but Billy's had a steering wheel, just like a car. You just don't waste dreams on something you know you are not going to get.

SLUDGE AND THE PITCHER PUMP

We had a cellar under the back porch, the pantry, bathroom, and water heater. It was a perfect storage room for Mom's home-canned vegetables, fruit, grape juice, and jelly. It was naturally cool because of the springs coursing under the cement floor. There was a brick-lined well under the dining room with an electric pump that pushed well water into the kitchen and bathroom sinks, the indoor convenience and the water heater.

The water for the tank was rainwater, and all the rain gutters on the house were routed to the cistern. There was a fairly large galvanized water storage tank in the attic that had sprung a leak. It was not repaired by the previous owner of the property, or Dad. There was a pitcher pump on the back porch and spigot. The way a pitcher pump works is similar to the working of a siphon. Our pump was attached to a concrete water storage tank buried in the yard outside the pantry. There was a cast-iron lid covering a large access hole on top of the tank. Buried galvanized pipes carried water from the tank to the washroom sink on the back porch. A stopper with a handle allowed you to screw down the stopper. You pumped down on the pump handle until the water filled the pipe. When you released the stopper there was enough pressure to pull the water out of the tank to the washroom. This description is probably wrong. I only saw one demonstration but the water forcefully spewed into the sink.

There was a catch basin ahead of the water storage tank and the catch basin was supposed to screen out leaves, small branches, seeds and sludge. Trouble was if nobody cleaned the catch basin, then the sludge was in the bottom of the water storage tank. I was twelve, old enough to siphon the water tank, but I also had to clean the sludge out of the tank with water buckets and a shovel; bucket by bucket full, wading through sludge. Sludge was squishy, smelly, rotten weeds and leaves, and dirty water.

SMALL TOWN PROFESSIONALS

The experience was and still is worth a trip to Paul Hill Cemetery in St. Paul. When I was a kid there weren't very many brave youngsters who would make the trip to the top, me included, without running for the decorative von gate with an all-out full-bore running dash if a hoot owl hooted and the feet noticeably accelerated on their own. Get caught up there in the dark and it was blacker than Dick's hat band. Make that trip someday for there are priceless grave markers, hand-carved by unknown artisans, one who carved a tree trunk with vines and open flowers creeping up and around the trunk. Think of it, those masons did not have an electronic chisel to smooth out the delicate work they produced by hand. Perhaps they honored their trade as it was done in Italy, Germany, Ireland, and the world as they knew it.

I can remember watching steel saw blades moving back and forth, back and forth with water dripping into the kerf to keep the blades cool, seeing these artisans creating their part of America the beautiful, stone windows and door sills, benches, bird baths.

Because America held out its hand to an anxious world yearning for its collective freedom to do its own thing, our America was the winner. Once in a while Europe sent its prejudices, too. However, our skin tones might be a tad different, but it doesn't have a thing to do with our collective abilities to get along together once we get the hang of it, to break bread together, to enjoy companionship, go to school, marry, talk over the back fence, work, just be friends, what in the world does it cost us? "Give us your…," as Poet Emma Lazarus said it! Read it. The world zero, America 100 percent.

STOKELY'S IN ST. PAUL

Stokely's canning factories bought out Mobley's canning factory. Bob Mitchell was brought in from Illinois as plant manager. The Mitchells took to St. Paul like a duck takes to water. When Bob bought Brunner Hardware, Goodyear tire store, and Standard oil filling station, Uncle Carl became Stokley's plant manager. Marianne Hawkins, a high school student, was his secretary whom he praised highly. Uncle Carl was one of the best one-finger typists I ever saw, but Marianne made that old Underwood sound like a machine gun.

SAINT PAUL CHRONICLES

Unless it was a one-street town, it seemed towns of any size platted in the old, old days, had two main intersecting streets, usually the business district, with east-west and north-south streets radiating from the main streets separating the blocks. Searching my memory for an incident I wanted to write about, the oddity of the platting of St. Paul came to mind. The east-west Decatur-Shelby county line road and the southeast northwest New York central RR Tracks bisect St. Paul. All houses built along the CLR on the Shelby CO-side face the County Line Road (CLR). Vinegar Hill was the local nickname for the west side of the RR Tracks. Two streets run parallel to the CLR with a middle connecting street at a right angle to the CLR. Houses on the third street face north, looking over a big open field. Goose Crick on the east side of the tracks, a more compact section, also parallels the CLR. Two streets on either side of the track converge just beyond "Mobley's" canning factory, into a five-mile road to Waldron. Six houses on the Decatur side of the CLR are built to face it. This construction and the platting of St. Paul created several triangular building lots. The Decatur side of St. Paul is platted on the bias to the New York Central tracks. Practically every block had necessary accesses to outbuildings, deliveries, garden plowing, shortcuts, the cleaning of outside conveniences, etc.

THE TEACHER

At the store, I would hear matronly customers talk about Mr. Nail, their Sunday school teacher. The class was so large they had their own Sunday school classroom. The way they talked I thought Dad was still teaching the class, but he trained enough potential teachers to keep the class going.

Didn't you know, your father taught our Sunday school class? Of course I didn't, but I liked Dad's style. When I was supervising a large crew in two widely separated buildings, I trained back-ups for all important jobs. Like actors, there was always someone in the wings ready to take over.

TEA TOWN

St. Paul must have been a tea-drinking community, because Dad bought the tea, picked and packed in heavy wooden boxes in the Orient. I remember quite well, it eventually became one of my jobs, and oh, the care we took, taking the lids off the wooden boxes and rolling back the foil and rice paper to get down to the loose tea. The first layer was lead foil apparently to keep out the vermin and water in case a box fell into the drink. Dad surmised that first layer to be lead because it was so heavy. Dad was the main surmiser. He was just about always right. The Master was never bested by the pupil. Then there were several layers of rice paper I peeled back one sheet at a time. Next came a layer of light-weight tinfoil, followed by several additional layers of rice paper, all meticulously fitted into the case, and then the tea, what a delicious odor.

They were salesmen, but in those days, they called them drummers and there were several that called on Dad. I think Dad got the tea from Johnson Brothers in Greensburg. I can remember Dad's store carrying the following varieties: Peko, Orange Peko, Ceylon and India; Gunpowder, Chinese green tea, the leaves rolled as it was picked, into pellets; Oolong, dark black tea, from China. Nowadays tea is grown in many other countries in the world where the growing conditions are right.

Dad experimented with mixing the teas to perfect his iced tea mix. He had customers coming to the store specifically to buy his iced tea mix. I do not remember Dad ever premixing a jar of the tea. If a customer asked for his iced tea mix, Dad would get out his Nichol-plated small-size scoop and create his magic from the boxes of teas lined up on the counter, as the customer watched. As I stated earlier, in a pinch I could mix a facsimile having watched the Master Mixer so many times. My mix was not as good as Dad's but it was drinkable.

TOM AND JACK

Maybe you noticed our pets didn't have genders. Generally, the way we got our pets was when they were walking by and stayed for Mom's fried-whatever supper.

A pretty little yellow-tiger kitten was rubbing her mark on Norma's ankles, who was trying to find the origin of the odor. Soon Norma's hand was getting a scrub down with a busy little pink tongue. No doubt about it, Tige had found his new home.

Truth of the matter was, our cats were usually Tom, Tommy, Ole Tom. So Tige adopted Norma; likely by eminent domain.

The name Jack was reserved for the dogs that happened to stroll by and became fond of Mom's table scraps. Those dumb dogs, in those days they didn't know chicken bones weren't healthy for dogs. They could dispose of a chicken skeleton in two or three unhealthy crunches.

And there was Tommy, Dad's cat! Dad's favorite sayings about his cat were: "Tommy wouldn't hurt a bird; Tommy wouldn't chase a bird." On one of those lazy Sunday afternoons, I was in the porch swing, Dad in his white rattan rocker, and Tommy was stretched out under Dad's chair, his tail perilously close to the rocker. Suddenly Tommy woke, stretched, jumped between the balustrades and strolled nonchalantly across the yard. As we watched, Tommy's fur stiffened. Tommy was doing one of his tail switching, belly to the ground, claws extended crawls towards an overweight chubby robin sitting under my car parked by the tall soft maple shade tree. We could see Tommy stiffen his leg muscles, ready to pounce. What a sly bird. He knew what Tommy had in mind and he flew into the shade tree. "I thought you said Tommy wouldn't chase a bird, Dad."

A nonplussed Dad thought a moment, and then responded, "They were just playing."

UNCLE CARL

Uncle Carl sold insurance. Dad insured the house, its contents, garage and the merchandise in the store. There was a wind-shear storm in St. Paul. Mom's weeping willow tree that grew in the yard by the garage had toppled into the garage. Dad had the damage repaired but he wouldn't file a claim with the insurance company because Uncle Carl was the agent and somehow the claim might count against Uncle Carl. Dad was loyal to his relatives.

VAN PELT BLOWOUT

There is a very popular swimming hole in Conns just above the place where it enters into the Flat Rock River and then takes a rather sharp bend, before the river turns placid again and heads off to eventually become a part of White River. I don't know if anyone special tried to keep the little rooting trees, shrubs, and berry vines cleaned out along Flat Rock.

Harve (I don't recall his actual name) was working along the banks of the Flat Rock. He had piles of debris stacked up that he was going to burn. Harve poured a thin stream of kerosene the length of the pile, and stuffed several old newspapers alongside it. Harve had noticed the rather strong scent of rotting vegetation. In some sections the odor was much stronger and Harve was getting a headache from inhaling the stench.

Harve picked up his dinner pail and headed for Conns Creek. When he got to the end of the trash, Harve stooped to light a newspaper. The fire really took off.

The explosion caught Harve as he was pouring a cup of hot coffee to go with his shepherd's pie. An accumulation of methane gas blew up just on the backside of the cemetery. Some of the coffins slid part way down the bluff. Other coffins were sticking partway out of the ground, resembling a giant pin cushion.

Excursion trains from Chicago, St. Louis, Cincinnati, and Columbus, Ohio came to St. Paul and Waldron. St. Paul had one hotel, rooming houses, restaurants, and taverns. Draymen made extra winter money hauling sightseers.

AND THAT WAS IT

Bucklin was a town farmer and lived in St. Paul. He rode out to the farm in his passenger car every day. Buck shipped most of what he raised on the farm in the Big Four Rail Road box cars. He would order a box car from one of the railroad agents that lived in St. Paul and get the car the next day. The car would be boarded and old jerk would pull the car to a county seat for immediate shipment via a freight train. Buck had a load that he wanted to go out post haste. He saw Charley Nitz, an agent. When Buck was in a big hurry, he could be really overbearing. "Charley, get me a box car in early for tomorrow morning. I have a load that has to go right away." Charley didn't like being ordered around by Buck and he put aside the paperwork. Buck was in town bright and early, asking, "Is my car in?"

"They must be low on empties, Buck, not yet." Buck was frantic. Charley told Dad about the delayed box car, He could have had the car in the same day Buck ordered it, but Buck wasn't going to order him to do so in that tone of voice. Charley made Buck wait a week. I was a witness to the exchange and knew when to keep my mouth shut!

Sometimes it was so simple to ship goods that the railroad workers would break the train and insert Buck's car right in the midst of the train.

THE VAN PELT CHURCH VICINITY

The Van Pelt country Church and Cemetery sits on a high bluff above Flat Rock River. Conns Creek that locals call Crick and Conns is a small tributary emptying into Flat Rock River where Flat Rock makes an elbow turn to flow south into White River.

Conns was a popular destination for picnickers or fishers. Dad would fish at Conns or Flat Rock. Mom and we kids would swim in Conns. Someone kept the grass, weeds, and seedlings mowed and regularly emptied the trash barrel. Youngsters within a large radius biked to Conns in their swimming suits.

Seemed like in those days, if you wanted to go fishing, mushrooming, or wild berry picking, you just went as long as the patch wasn't cultivated or visibly maintained. If you saw someone near the house or barn, you told them your name and asked for picking permission. In some big patches you could fill a water bucket in minutes. I liked to go berrying with James and Eddy Wise. They knew where the best patches were. They filled their buckets faster than I did. They were patient waiting for me to finish. About half the time, if just Eddy and I were going and Eddy was still in bed, Mrs. Wise would let me go upstairs and roust him out.

For about a week or two James and Eddy would walk down the road to their church for catechism. Then James went to Cincinnati for special training, but he flunked out and came back home. Leonard was the apple of the Wise family's eye. Leonard played the trumpet and beautiful music played on that trumpet entertained St. Paul almost every evening. Leonard was killed in the European Theater Operation overseas, WWII. It was like a much-loved tree had been cut down. I think everybody in St. Paul felt the loss. Such a waste.

VERY LATE ON SATURDAY NIGHT

Saturday night, actually Sunday morning, and just minutes after 2:00 a.m., the last farmer would come into the store. All evening he'd nursed two or three bottles of Blue Ribbon and a cellophane sack of salted peanuts at the tavern. Old cronies together did a lot of plowing, told yarns, pulled weeds, and shared possum in the hen house stories; farmer talk. There'd be sleepy little tykes to carry out of the family car to their warm beds. One of the Nail boys had loaded the groceries and the farmer's new bib overalls in the trunk.

WATER STORAGE TANKS

About all the downspouts on the house were routed to the water storage tank (WST). There was a catch basin just ahead of the pipe to the WST. The catch basin was supposed to screen out leaves, small branches, seeds and sludge. Trouble was if nobody dumped the catch basin then all that sludge was in the bottom of the WST. At twelve I was old enough to clean the WST. (Thank goodness for Honey Dippers. I think I would have become a twelve-year-old hobo if that job had befallen me.) About that WST job: Nobody ever emptied the catch basin.

THE 1935 DROUGHT

During the 1935 drought, Flat Rock River nearly went dry. We could walk across the river at the riffles without getting our shoes wet. Downriver from the railroad bridge was a beautiful three-arch limestone bridge built by Civil War veteran Ed Eck. His brother Joe mined the rock for the bridge downriver from the location of the bridge. The river flowed under the middle arch; there was a rough fisherman's driveway under the nearer arch. A railroad spur sat next to Greely's limestone quarry and crusher on the far side of the river under the third arch. The last time I had visions of crossing the stone-arch bridge, I was coming towards St Paul from Germantown and that beautiful white bridge had been replaced with a modern cement structure. Wouldn't it have been great if that beautiful arch bridge was left as a walking bridge for bicyclists? I wonder when was the last time I saw railroad cars loaded with crushed stone threading their way under that arch with the engineer sending plumes of black coal smoke smudging purposely—the last time I saw that ancient building white limestone, or the last time I walked or biked it. I walked the rails with Eddy and Jimmy Wise, Billy Alter, Gus Leffler, the Townsend boys, John and Dick Young, Tater McKee, the Thornburg boys; we all met there!

WHO'S TOM THUMB?

We were working in the garden. Keefy, a neighborhood boy, hurried down the alley. "Miz Nail, can I use your turlit?" Keefy asked, reaching for the black ceramic doorknob to the convenience.

"Yes, Keefy," as the boy disappeared through the door. A relieved Keefy said, "Thanks, Miz Nail," as he fastened the other strap of his bib overalls. Keefy walked leisurely, the two blocks towards his home.

Mom always allowed a place in the garden for Tom Thumb (miniature sized corn). Mom planted it so it couldn't cross the country gentleman sweet corn. Mom left a basket in the garden to pick it. I would lay them on the kitchen table. Mom picked the best for next year's crop. One of Tom Thumb's characteristics, each single grain on the short ear had a needle-sharp point on the end. I always tried to find tightly closed spaced grains on the ear rub, and the others with a tight one and grain would rattle into the pan. Generally I'd do the next year's crop first so Mom could put it into a tight container stored in a safe place, then I'd do the rest. When I was working with Tom Thumb I carefully separated it from the woody core; even so, I still had bruised, cut and punctured hands and fingers. Tom Thumb was worth it, it was the best. To my taste, Black Jewel is too dry and the hybrids, genetically monkeyed-with, are ok, I guess. Leon loved Tom Thumb. He'd put lots of pepper in his to keep Norma and me from trying to get some of it. We didn't put pepper in our Tom Thumb; instead we generously shared our popcorn. Weren't Norma and I two little diamonds in the rough? My brother, Leon, was Norma's dad (Pop).

THE WORD

More than likely, the family Bible was one of Dad's textbooks. Dad was partial to the King James Version, mainly because that translation was about the only translation available. Dad praised King James for the poetry renditions of the Psalms and Proverbs. Dad could quote verbatim long favorite passages. I would hear matronly customers talk about Dad, their Sunday school teacher. Apparently, when Dad moved the family to St. Paul, like Mom teaching potential swimming partners how to swim, he taught the town women about the Bible. I don't know whether Dad took over an existing teacher's class for Mom's sake, to please her. Neither do I know how long Dad was the teacher for the ladies' class, but it must have been for quite some time, because even after Dad gave the job to a new teacher, older former students still praised Mr. Nail, their beloved teacher. I wonder if Dad, the former teacher, taught his replacement.

Gova, Perton, and Sherman Early 1940s

Sherman Nail with his dog, Old Betty, 1953

Mary Alice on J.K.'s 'new' bike Approx. 1935

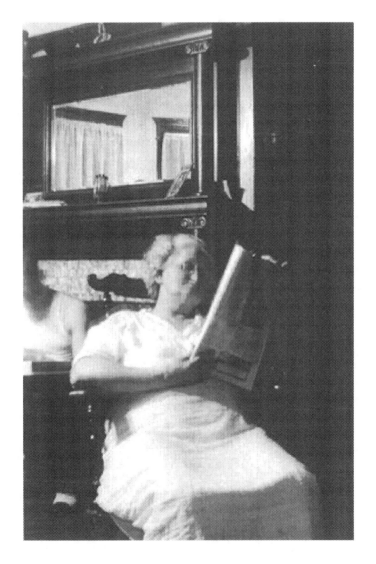

Mary Alice reading the newspaper Approx. 1935

Leon and Adrian Nail as children Approx. 1906

Evelyn and Doris Nail Approx. 1912

Marian, Doris, Evelyn, and James Nail (in front) Approx. 1926

Leon, Doris, Julian, Marian, Adrian, James, Evelyn Approx. 1925

Gova and Auvie Naile Approx. 1925

Adrian Nail Approx. 1935

K of P Building, site of Nail & Co. store, Approx. 1935

James Naile and Norman Wolverton at Nail & Co. store Approx. 1935

J.K. Nail in his Army Air Corp portrait 1943

Norman Wolverton and Sherman Nail in
the rear of the store Approx. 1945

Aunt Sadie in the flower garden Approx. 1945

Betty Lou Satterfield (Engagement photo 1947)

J.K. and Betty Nail at the St. Paul house 1948

Sherman in yard with Leah Jane Approx. 1953

Judy family by the church 2006

Marian Judy, J.K. Nail, James Naile, Evelyn Steiner,
Virginia White, Doris Wolverton, Leon Nail 1997

1997 Nail Family Reunion picture 1997

1998 Nail Reunion picture 1998

J.K.and Betty Nail, and Marian Judy at the Nails 2006

Mary Lou and Marian Judy, J.K. and Betty Nail 2007

J.K. at the kitchen table 2013

The St. Paul house where J.K. and his
brothers and sisters grew up 2016

The St. Paul, Indiana welcome sign 2016

PERSONAL EXPERIENCE STORIES AND NOTES (POST WWII)

THE BOMB

Bill and his family lived in Greater Cincinnati over the Ohio River in Ludlow, Kentucky. Bill worked for the Post Office; his primary job was handling registered mail on a Railway Post Office (RPO). On duty, Bill carried a holstered six-shot, for safety, one chamber empty, Smith and Wesson Bankers Special revolver. Bill was tested yearly for firearm proficiency, which was a little like hitting a cow in the south end of one while walking north. As long as you hit in or near the target's concentric circles, you passed. Bill carried an LA key (a universal postal key) to open the regular locks on sacks and pouches, and a special key to open heavy-duty padlocks on registered mail pouches. He carried the keys on a knee-length chain fastened to his leather belt. In his wallet was his official railroad pass authorizing the bearer to ride any train departing either terminus of his assigned run or any train that would get him to Chicago before his train had departed, and/or back to Chicago at the end of the run.

Bill left Ludlow, Kentucky to deadhead to Chicago to catch his run on the New York Central (NYC) Chicago and Cincinnati, Chic and Cin pronounced chick and sin. On the Departure board, the departure time was set back for an indeterminate length of time to wait for a special piece of registered mail. No one had a clue as to what or why it was so special.

At last an engine pushing an ordinary nondescript storage car appeared on the NYC track and attached the storage car to the waiting Railway Post Office (RPO). Bill verified the identification number on the item to the paperwork and copied them into his Registry Logbook. He signed the papers, accepting responsibility for the item and acknowledging receipt.

Suspended in the center of the storage car, in a spider web of chains emanating from every conceivable point, was a steel box. In a worst-case scenario, for example, a train wreck, broken wheel, or hot box, the steel box, with an origin of University of Illinois, Chicago, the destination of Oak Ridge, Tennessee, would arrive intact and undamaged just as it had been when it was signed for by a Hoosier RPO Registered Mail Clerk, Bill Hurst, from my hometown, St. Paul, Indiana.

EARLY POSTAL DAYS

I think reorganizing twice a year was unique to the Railway Mail Service (RMS) and that didn't change when I joined the Postal Transportation Service (PTS) in 1949. The twice yearly reorgs followed along. Reorg had happened in the spring when the requested two new runs (jobs) were awarded. I was senior to Merle Bosh and I took the day job and Merle went to late nights. The two new runs would be on the autumn reorg so my days on the day shift were numbered.

The Air Mail Facility (AMF) supervisors worked the pouch rack and whoever subbed for them was generally the acting supervisor. There were four supervisors. Newman Davis was ensconced on Tour One (midnight shift). Newman liked his coffee so strong that when he made a pot, he could whistle, and the pot would walk over and fill his cup. And so sweet to the point it was cheaper to buy sugar in 100 lb. sacks. You could hear Newman stirring the sugar in his cup so loud it drowned out the radio. One of the Tour One clerks brought in a spoon handle without the bowl. When Newman poured a cup of coffee and sugared it, it made no difference to him if the cup of coffee was blistering hot or ice cold, he would eventually drink it. His ritual included re-stirring the coffee when he sat down at the desk. The trickster substituted the handle for the spoon. All the guys were watching Newman when he started stirring with the handle. He pulled the handle out with an odd look. Someone said, "I knew that coffee was going to eat that spoon someday!"

Cal Phillips was Supt. of the AMF on Tour Two (Day shift). I liked working the pouch rack and he let me. It was strange, me, the junior clerk, supervising Beck and Virg. Our days off were Sunday and Monday.

FLYBOY BURGETT

Robert Burgett, an experienced pilot, had hundreds of hours of flight experience. During WWII, Bob was an Allison Engine Company Field Representative. He moved from field to field, possibly continent to continent, to troubleshoot and survey the performance of aircraft with Allison liquid cooled engines, P-38, P-39, and P-41. They saw combat early in the war, but later were used mainly in reconnaissance because of their speed and high altitude capabilities.

After WWII ended, Bob's representative duties ceased. Bob, in my recollection, became a wholesaler of kitchen cabinets, appliances, etc. for the building trades. Bob owned his own plane. On a hunting trip with a friend to the Dakotas, it was theorized that Bob was disoriented when he flew into a fog bank. The instrument that tells the pilot when he is flying straight and level could not differentiate between horizontal and vertical. The report stated that Bob flew straight down into an Indiana farm field. Bob left a wife and infant daughter. I have read that the instrument is still unstable and unchanged in some personal aircraft.

Several years ago, a similar accident happened to a well-known Hoosier pilot and family with guest passengers, a popular restaurateur and his family, whose plane crashed in Kentucky under similar circumstances. And in reality, this very set of circumstances could have contributed to the accident in which Major Glen Miller, of the WWII era, a very popular band leader, lost his life. If the weather in the Glen Miller movie is correct, then it fits the profile of the two above accidents. Since no wreckage was found, did the Norse single-engine plane nosedive into the North Atlantic Ocean or the English Channel?

HALIBUT

How about a one-day open season just to catch a one-fish limit in the Bering Sea? Fortunately for Betty and me, the restaurant near Denali National Park, where we were eating our evening meal, had bought a good-size piece of the fresh-caught halibut that just barely fit in the bed of a standard wide-bed pickup truck.

HOW HOT WAS IT?

An article in *The Indianapolis Star* stated a few more entries were wanted for the annual World Champion Liar contest. Indiana should be a veritable gold mine for the contest. Besides the "no increase in taxes" state and national Indiana politicians, there are numerous amateur truth stretchers, me included. I thought I'd share a far-fetched, nearly true story. Enclosed is the no-entry fee of $1—no kidding.

My wife, Betty, and I are amateur photographers. We saved our money for a ten-day African Photo Safari to see and photograph the wild animals in their natural habitat. The first one and a half days of the trip were spent getting to Africa and the Safari base camp. Meeting our guide and fellow photographers for orientation took up the afternoon. The last day would be spent getting back to the airport for our flight home. This left seven days for taking pictures. It seemed our cameras ran continuously. All manner of animals indigenous to the area were out in force, all, that is, except the elusive lions, which roared all night and hid all day. Our guide bolstered our hopes by sending native trackers into the bush looking for lions. You know how we Midwesterners enjoy those 50° below low pressure front Albert Clippers in January.

On day five, we were eating our evening meal when the temperature began to rise perceptibly. The guide called the phenomena an Equatorial Juggernaut high pressure stationary heat-wave front. The temperature topped out at 47°C (125°F). Day six was a wipe out. No self-respecting animal was about to give up a speck of shade to pose for pictures. Day seven, without abatement in the heat wave, the guide roused us at 2:00 a.m. for a light breakfast before our final Land Rover trip to a shooting blind situated on a waterhole trail. As he drove, the guide reiterated his rules of no talking, eating, tobacco products, or noise of any kind. In the blind, we set up our cameras in advantageous positions and sat down to wait. With the first streaks of light we were poised at our cameras. Dawn and right in front of our blind was a lion chasing an impala. It was so hot, they were both walking.

AN ALARMING EXPERIENCE

Betty and I attended about twenty-five Elderhostel Programs. We found them quite interesting and educational. One Program we attended was in an abandoned logging camp north of Kalispell, Montana. Talk about rustic, that's where the word rustic originated. The men were in one building; the ladies in another. Lights went out at 9:00 at night, when the generator kicked off; back on in the morning at 6:00. Breakfast was at 7:00. Two occupants to a room. I was lucky enough to get a fellow with an alarm clock and a penchant for being roused at an early hour then resetting the clock and going back for another hour of sleep. As for me, on the other hand, whatever time the alarm clock goes off, I'm bright-eyed and out of bed. Anybody who has a notion that the beds in an empty logging camp are going to be goose-down feather soft, please take an air mattress with you.

One morning my roommate forgot to put his alarm clock away. Tired of early morning rousing, I reset the clock for six. Did he notice the next morning that I was just getting up and dressing and the lights were on or that his alarm clock matched the automatic official lights on time? Nah, he reset his clock up one hour and went back to sleep. He never said anything about his late breakfast or technically his extra two hours of sleep instead of one, and his alarm always went back in his suitcase. The last day of the program, we shook hands, lied to each other by saying, "Nice meeting and talking to you," and pulled out of the parking lot.

Elderhostel Customs: We had enjoyed some of the best lecturers we had ever heard. We now had a much better knowledge of what clear cut was and reseeding immense areas were. We saw virgin trees that lumber companies were itching to cut. We got graduation certificates and the cooks outdid themselves, while the BYOBers livened up their conversations as the dregs disappeared. Miss on the Hunt was trailing an interested live one. I think the girls were urging her on; the guys nolens volens. That's life!

FROM HIBEN AND HOLLEWEG TO EASTERN

James and I shared a mutual friend. James and he were friends at Hiben and Holleweg Drygoods Wholesale House in Indianapolis.

I don't recall his name, but he and I worked together moving vast quantities of airmail. He was a Ramp Agent for Eastern Airlines and I worked air mail at the Weir Cook Airport. Generally Eastern could handle all the transfer mail to Chicago and we loaded it on.

PRANKS AND THANKS

You might not know it, but these military men are those same mischievous boys who took the stone pillar out from under the corner of the schoolhouse. In just a few years, they would take apart a big farm wagon, carry the pieces up on the top of the barn, and reassemble the wagon over the ridge pole, back when the rite of Halloween was fun time. Somebody's shotgun might boom, but did you notice the tiny bird shot rattled down the galvanized roof in a safe place? If they got caught, they didn't care. Chances are, the farmer who caught them remembered Old Man So-n'-so had caught them when he too had moved a wagon up on a barn roof.

Look around! These are the gray beards whose sons hit the beaches on Guadalcanal, Saipan, Iwo Jima, Utah, Omaha; jumped out of airplanes, were dragged to war in flimsy boxes, towed there behind passenger airplanes turned into war birds that hurried back to Britain after being the platform for the jumpers to get their brave brethren, the airborne infantry, or they went to sea in every conceivable conveyance mankind could dream up. Maybe they are your mother's kid brother, your uncle, your grandfather, that old man messing around in a postage stamp-size garden, raising the sweetest garden tomatoes. Don't you agree?

THE RED STONE PEACE PIPE

I don't know why I was chosen to preserve the Red Stone Peace Pipe, mentioned earlier. I got the Pipe in Pipe Stone National Monument in Pipestone, MN. It has been in repose, undisturbed on the fireplace mantel in our home for as long as I was its caretaker. No one really owns a Red Stone Peace Pipe. As it should, it passes from generation to generation, friend to friend. What I am pointing out is the reverence in which the native Indian placed in the beauty in which they lived. They settled their differences over a red stone peace pipe. Would these first settlers to this land have been so bloodthirsty if they had not been taught warring and scalping by the Europeans who took advantage of them?

I know there are groups here in Indiana that have petitioned the Federal Government for decades to receive recognition as legitimate tribes, to no avail. I decided I wanted my pipe to go to a family who would pay the pipe the respect it deserved, a family who would relish its presence in their home, a family with a descendant. It seems I have known and been a friend of Bill and Pat Proctor forever and a day. Bill Proctor is an American native Indian, a decorated Nam, Silver Star, veteran, a descendant of eastern Canada Indians. Like Allstate's TV ad, my Red Stone Peace Pipe is in Good Hands.

Don't you wish we all had Red Stone Peace Pipes? Maybe we could settle our differences, difficulties and tiffs with a Red Stone Peace Pipe just like our Indian brothers have done.

ENGLISH HOWARDS?

In Florence, Italy Betty and I were seated on a park bench in front of an ancient church, under reconstruction renovation. There were two English couples on an adjacent bench.

"Americans?" one of the men inquired.

At my acquiescence, he continued, "Of English descent?"

"Well, I know of German descent in our family. My mother was very proud of her French descent. Dad said we were of Welsh descent. There is bound to be English blood somewhere."

"What was your grandmother's maiden name?"

"Howard."

"That is my name, too. Do you know anything about the Howards?"

To my "No," he continued, "Half of the Howards were Protestants. The other half were Catholic. The Protestants stayed in Wales. The Catholics moved East near Dover. They are still there. The King wanted to divorce his wife and the Pope said no. The King disavowed the Pope and chased a lot of the Catholics away."

Our tour bus pulled up and we had to leave. I sure would have liked to talk some more with my newfound relative.

WHAT'D SHE SAY?

Visiting Mobile, Betty and I were standing in a cafeteria line behind a young couple. Their children had selected Jell-o, the mother chose slaw. The sixtyish salad lady was holding a tossed salad. She Deep-Southerned something towards the father. "Beg pardon?" he New-Jerseyed. The lady repeated what she had said. The father replied, "Did you?" as his wife shook her head. I tapped him on the arm, "She wants to know if you want French, Thousand Island, Ranch, poppy seed or blue cheese". The line bunched near the cashier. The fellow turned towards me to ask, "Are you from around here?" "No, we're from Indiana." As he turned away, I thought his look said, "Hicks!"

Recently, I read an article about WWII radio operators. The author said the military in all branches of the services preferred, when possible, their radio operators to be from the Midwest. It is probably because if we have a discernible regional accent, it is as thin and flat as beef patties in a cut-rate hamburger joint. I guess most everybody can understand what we say regardless of what it is because our speech is plain old, melting-pot American English.

YE REAP WHAT I SEW

I thought I should finish my green thumb stories. I believe I have been known to plant various other seeds in other flower pots, the plants getting yanked out before maturity. Wayne, Postal Div. Controller, to brighten his office, brought in a big redwood planter filled with low-growing greenery. Anytime Wayne was out of the office I filled in for him. One winter we were eating grapefruit for breakfast every morning. I saved the seeds for the birds, which quickly dropped them out of the feeder for the squirrels, which also turned up their noses at this new fare. For little critters that bury nuts all over kingdom come, they would have come nearer to burying a VW Beetle than they would a grapefruit seed. I can't understand how their brain functions. They'd climb through 10" of axle grease to get to the sunflower seeds and not even cut open a citrus seed to see if it was edible. Wayne was out of the office and I planted two grapefruit seeds in his planter. Now those grapefruit seeds loved this new environment and soon put up a couple of shoots, which, with all the other plants there, you couldn't see. It must been around the first of March when I walked into Wayne's office and saw he and his secretary staring at the planter because by now we were getting growing action. Those slender trees, with dark-green leaves glistening, stood about six inches above their planter companions. I sidled up to the planter to help them look at the "trees." Wayne to Barb, "When I bought the plants, the nursery assured me they would all be the same height." "I can't imagine why those two are growing so tall," said she, and paused, then with an afterthought, looking at me, asked, "Can you?" I always lay claim to my capers, so I answered, "Sure, those are grapefruit trees." Almost in unison, "How could grapefru—, JK!" It must have been along about then when I gave up on indoor gardening.

YES, THERE WAS A POOL OF BLOOD

No, not in New York, in Chicago. I was summoned to come to Chicago along with almost everybody else, it seemed, for a Postal Service meeting at Division Headquarters. Dinner was running late, so the bar was opened. Finally dinner was to be served. The waitress set a plate in front of me. It was a raw piece of meat swimming in a pool of blood. They noticed I was eating the salad. I asked if she would take the meat back, pour the blood down the drain and cook the meat. "Ah, the meat has been cooked, Sir." Sometimes things roll off my tongue that I wish I hadn't said. "Oh, Really? I wish the cook had turned the burner under the skillet on high. I am not going to eat this raw meat." She winked at me and picked up the plate. Glad I ate the salad.

After WWII, that meal we were served when we got back to the States was good. That was the first T-bone steak I ever ate and it was actually cooked the way Mom would have fried it. Oh, she would have served it with brown gravy, more than likely, and with mashed potatoes. But it was well-done. I had never eaten meat in the Mess Hall that wasn't cooked well-done. What had got into the Army cooks? Surely I wasn't the only one who wanted the meat cooked all the way through, was I??

STORIES (AND NOTES OF EVENTS)
THAT WERE PASSED DOWN

TRAGEDY AT THE TRACK

I heard Dad repeat this story to numerous gatherings of people in those days, especially on Memorial Day weekends when races were running in Indianapolis.

"Morning, Sherm," said Homer. "Mind if we wait in here until Old Jerk gets back from Martinsville? It's chilly outside."

Old Jerkwater was the affectionate nickname for the local trains that stop at every town coming and returning on the spur lines to and from the main railroad lines. Many new engineers cut their teeth, so to speak, and learned trade on the locals and spur lines. Old Jerk was the passenger, freight, mail, paper boy, train running southwest from Fairland to Franklin, Trafalgar, Morgantown, Martinsville and back. Like farm families living close to the spur, you could flag down old Jerk, pay a fare and ride to town or terminus. I have ridden trains in Alaska and Canada that have that kind of service, or they did when we were there.

"Where are you boys going, Homer?"

"Oh, I'm going to Indianapolis to see some fool get killed in that automobile race at the new motor speedway track."

The 300-mile race would be run on a track constructed of crushed stone, covered with a thick coat of hot asphalt on a heavy base of compacted clay.

During the race the track began to break up and there were some pot holes beginning to form. But the race continued. It was nearing the time to catch the train to Fairland, so the boys left their seats, headed for the gate.

Homer told his companions, "Go ahead, I'll catch up with you. I want to look at something." An unknown something, the boys would say later.

There was a low dirt barrier around the track, and an open space behind the barrier, which track security was working diligently at, trying to keep the onlookers out. And it was into this space Homer arrived.

A race car coming into the turn hit a pot hole and blew the right front tire. The race car went airborne and landed where Homer was standing, killing him instantly. The riding mechanic fell to his death from the soaring race car, and the race car was demolished.

On August 21, 1909, Homer Jolliffe of Trafalgar, Indiana and James West of Indianapolis became the first two spectators killed in an accident at the new Indianapolis Motor Speedway. It took a driver injury—scalp lacerations from flying rocks—that fateful Saturday afternoon before the race was stopped with twenty-six laps to go.

1816—THE WINTER IN THE SUMMER

The way Dad talked about the second week of June 1816, I thought he had lived through it. An impossibility; he was born November 27, 1871. (Dad soaked up stories like a new sponge, stories to retell to those family members interested and eager to hear, like his youngest son, for instance, Julian, me.)

I learned the weather phenomenon occurred the second week of June 1816 as he learned from his parents David and Mary Nail who learned it from their parents John and Rachel Nail. In 1816 John would have been fifteen to sixteen years old, Rachel, eleven to twelve. (On August 09, 1821, sixteen-year-old Rachel married twenty-one-year-old John Nail.)

At those ages, both would have had a very good grasp of weather conditions, hardships, foodstuff availability or lack of, and the ability of domestic and wild animals to fend for themselves.

I don't remember whether I heard it on TV or read it, but there was speculation that the summer in the winter had been caused by the Ring of Fire. It may have been someone's theory but it seemed plausible. All the Ring of Fire was released almost simultaneously. The debris of this action getting into the jet stream was so great that it produced a sun-blocking drape almost all the way around the world. Communications at that time being what they were, knowledge of such a happenstance would be slow in the telling.

This extraordinary weather phenomenon occurred starting from a day in the second week of June 1816 and continuing until its exodus a few days later.

The second week of June began just like all weeks usually begin, except this week did not meet its usual criteria. For one thing, spring was not its usual self. It was the weather or it wasn't. The first storm was the usual skiff (colloquial: very small lightweight snow).

The early snow had come and gone. It turned cold and began snowing again. By the time the last flake of the freakish storm landed, twenty inches of snow covered Indiana and eighteen other states. It was bitter cold. Streams and ponds were frozen nearly solid. Lakes and rivers were freezing. The storm that spawned the snow lingered on like an uninvited guest.

Winter wheat and hearty garden seed would have been planted, if the signs were right, in the autumn of 1815 for the spring gardens. In normal times, the stalks of wheat would have been pulled together in manageable bundles and tied with hemp thins or a few strands of stems and stood upright together in shocks with bundles on top of the shocks, to siphon the water away if it rained. When the shocks were dry and the grain would fall away easily from its husk, it was time to beat out the grain from its husk with a flail. The winter wheat planted the previous fall in 1815 would have been harvested in the spring months of March, April, and in May. In June it would be in shocks drying for the winnowing.

But now, the winter wheat was immediately dead on its frozen stems. The gardens were lost to the freeze. Fruit orchards were frozen to ruination.

It was great the ladies had so diligently filled the cellar larder; carryover food such as dried, pickled, precooked and canned, was safe and edible and was parceled out to stretch meals when the usual garden food would not be available this stingy year. (Dad remembered watching his mom sealing pickles in earthenware and catsup in bottles with a bright red sealing wax that had to be heated to liquefy it. The wax had a distinctive, clean odor. His mom saved the used red wax to be recycled another year.)

Seed corn laid aside for this year's planting, if properly stored, could be saved for planting in 1817.

Wild game would feel this crazy weather just as the people did. Perhaps they opened ice in the deep lakes for the fish trapped there.

While there would be no corn to save this strange 1816 year, how it would have been harvested in a normal season is worth the telling. The corn would have been planted in hills; the hills were created by hand with a hoe.

During the year without a summer, put yourself into the shoes of our ancestors. A family to feed, forage animals to feed, wheat, corn, vegetable, staples gone for this year. "What will we do?"

SHOELESS, AND THE FICE

I really did try to go shoeless, but I was never able to hack it. I think my feet would have hidden in the pockets of my denim bib overalls, if I had tried walking on gravel, crushed stone, mowed grass, stiff weeds, blackberry and raspberry brambles, and yearly spring hot-liquid macadam applied to all streets in St. Paul. Kerosene was the only thing that would cut the tar. Some kids had to wear out their tar soles because their parents hid the precious oil in the little coal oil can. That oil was saved to quick-start the cook stove and for evening house lights. Potatoes were so cheap that a small potato was the spout stopper in most coal oil cans.

Sometimes, if we were swimming on a tar day, we'd get trapped at the falls. I sure can tell you some of us walked a country mile to get to our shoes at the Falls then back home without getting our feet and shoes oily. Some kids would build plank and flat rock bridges. You had to be careful on the rock bridge. Hit the rocks wrong and you'd be sitting in hot tar.

In Dad's childhood, during the Great Depression, when spring arrived, some adults and practically all children doffed their shoes, to be saved for late fall and winter use when they were sorely needed. It is hard to image Dad going barefoot even as a youngster. I'd seen others wade through shattered glass, brambles, stiff-stemmed weeds and the like. Dad was four going on five when the following incident happened.

Someone had dropped a Ball Mason green canning jar in the yard, up near the farmhouse. However, they failed to pick up the broken glass. Young Sherman, running and playing, stepped squarely on the thick glass jar bottom with some upright shards still attached; his little foot was pierced. His screams of pain and fright brought his mother on the run. Mary C. whipped off her apron, wrapped it around his foot to slow down the spouting bloody discharge and carried the youngster into the house.

From the tutelage of her mother, Lucinda, she knew which wild medicinal plants to pick and preserve for future use. Turpentine and fat bacon were in her home remedies arsenal. Don't laugh, our mother had similar skills. I have had deep-driven splinters trying to avoid the drawing powers of fat bacon and turpentine eased out slicker than a whistle.

I do not know whether Mary C. performed all the medical chores or if Dad had some professional medical help, too, or if it was available.

Since Sherman could not walk, his mother prepared a pallet on which he could rest. She carried the pallet out and placed it and young Sherman under a shade tree for the medicinal qualities of fresh air and sunlight. She unwrapped the dressing on the wound. Dad's words, "When the dressing came off the wound, the fice would rush over to lick the matter out of the exposed wound." (Fice, a general term for a family's pet dog.) Dad always claimed that the dog, by keeping the wound clean, was responsible for the quick healing of the wound. Of course Grandmother Mary C. was schooled in home-prepared family medicines as was our mother, Mary Alice.

THE SETTLERS, AS TOLD BY MY FATHER

When the settlers came into Johnson County, wild game, fish and edible plants were plentiful. Dad could remember seeing land suitable for farm fields being cleared for raising grain, livestock, and poultry, and for kitchen gardens. Dad could also remember seeing the obstacles that blocked their way. He described first-growth virgin trees cut down, the diameter of the stumps so great that (Dad's words) a full-grown man could lie across the stump and neither his head or his feet would hang over the edges. Dad was talking about native hardwood trees such as black and white walnut, beech, oak, yellow poplar, and maple. Some of the trees reached the height of 120 feet. A few of the trees listed above as hardwood are not, but they were prized for other reasons. There would be very little undergrowth simply because of the over crown of the taller trees.

At the time of the clearing, the settlers would use as much of the timber as possible, for firewood, shelter, fencing and outbuildings, even boats if near a pond, lake or river. There was not a market for the surplus. When they were clearing the land, as best they could they felled those trees in piles to burn them. Of course the wood they used would have to be cured to build home cabins, log outbuildings, and lean-tos.

NOTE: White Walnut is also called Pig Nut. During World War I, White Walnut trees were cut nearly to extinction because of the demand for their use as airplane propellers.

THE WAR OF 1812-1816

As told to my father, Sherman Nail, born on November 27, 1871, by his father, David Nail, born October 11, 1846 in Brown County, Indiana. David being the son of John Nail, born January 1, 1795 and Rachel Johns Nail, born March 13, 1805, both in Pennsylvania, and as told to me by my father, Sherman. John Nail was a veteran of the War of 1812; John's father, Henry, served in the American Revolution.

The skirmishers were tired. It was a long, full-pack hike. Would they never reach a defensible bivouac here in northern Ohio? From time to time, an officer would lead a trooper out for picket duty. Seventeen-year-old John Nail was posted in an oak thicket for night picket duty.

The sun was setting towards the horizon. He had his Pennsylvania-forged 0.50 caliber smooth bore, forty-and-one-half-inch, shaped octagon-to-round barrel rifle, lying across his thighs, his thumb at the on or near the hammer.

The original flintlock ignition system had been converted to percussion cap. The rifle was fitted with a brass patch box for the patches and percussion cap and a small container of grease. The rifle had the earmarks of meticulously fine Pennsylvania construction. Craftsman's pride was displayed in the brass-mounted, curly maple stock. John was well armed for the task ahead.

Grandfather was seated, leaning against an elderly lightning-hit oak in a small copse of seedlings. The ground under the tree was littered with acorns. John could hear the contented grunting of a wild pig searching in the leaves for the plump acorns. Perhaps young John was downwind of the hog, for it seemed the animal was slowly approaching him. John thought roasted pork would surely liven up a meal tomorrow. The guys would certainly relish a change from the old standard salt pork, the fatty part from the backs, sides and belly of a hog cured in salt, and the usual evening meal for tired soldiers on the march from their last bivouac.

First things first: powder horn, lead ball, patches, ramrod; check the flint, the steel, powder in the pan. He lifted the rifle to his shoulder, carefully aimed the weapon towards the scuffling sounds, and loosed a ball in that direction. There was not a sound from the porker, no thrashing about, no footfalls retreating from the scene, nothing. John told his listeners he was sure he'd hit the pig.

As the sun filtered through the tree branches the next morning, within thirty-five feet of John lay a dead Indian, a factory-manufactured cast iron tomahawk in an outstretched hand; a razor-sharp knife near the other. An important ally of his British masters.

WINTER WHEAT

Winter wheat: any of several cereal grasses having dense erect spikes bearing husks containing bread wheat grains. The 1815 seed would be planted in the fall for the 1816 growing season.

The grain grass was cut by hand using a cradle scythe, a farm tool with a long, single-edge blade set at an angle on a long, curved handle, with a frame fastened to the scythe so the cut grain could be laid evenly as it was cut. The cut grain was gathered and tied into bundles that were stacked upright with a few bundles on top to form a rain runoff roof over the shocks.

When the shocks were dry and the grain would fall easily from the husk, cotton sheets were laid out on which to flail the grain. A flail is a farm tool consisting of a free-swinging stick tied to the end of a long handle used to thresh the grain by hand. In the winnowing, the chaff would blow away, leaving the wheat grains.

Once again, during the year with the winter in the summer, put yourself into the shoes of our ancestors. A family to feed, forage animals to feed, wheat, corn, vegetable, staples gone for the year. "What could we do?"

PASSENGER PIGEONS

Passenger Pigeon: a variety of North American pigeons with a narrow tail longer than its wings. Formerly abundant, there was a wholesale, systematic slaughter of the passenger pigeon toward extermination in 1914. According to Dad's recollection, there were millions of passenger pigeons in single flocks. On the wing, a flock of the birds could make a lengthy blackout of the sun as they passed overhead.

The preferred food of the Passenger Pigeon was soft-shell nuts. The locations of the nut trees were embedded in their brains, for they followed the nut-ripening schedule. They shucked and consumed beechnut, chestnut, buckeye, soft-shell hickory nuts, acorns, pecans, pignuts, etc. If you have never had the opportunity to try pignuts, I highly recommend it. The nut looks like a small hickory nut. I would be remiss if I did not warn you, the pignut is as bitter as gall.

Since there was a lucrative market for Passenger Pigeons, a standard procedure for hunting the birds was developed. Large string nets were knit with openings large enough to allow the bird's head and neck to protrude through the openings, but too small for the passage of the bodies and wings. The pigeon hunters suspended quick-release nets in the lower branches of the nut trees, with the birds gathering into a feeding frenzy. When sufficient birds were feeding, the nets were released. Although the birds were trapped, they stuck their heads up through the netting and continued frantically feeding. The docile pigeons were oblivious to the hunters stomping through the crowded birds, snapping the birds' necks as they progressed forward. In order to harvest the kill, the nets had to be hoisted back up under the branches so the dead birds would fall out of the nets or could be pulled through.

Finally, the birds were packed in layers in coarse rock salt in oak barrels. Draymen hauled the barrels to railheads. The barrels were freighted to all the major cities in North America. As per Dad, some may have been shipped overseas on fast ocean liners.

Finally, mankind in his infinite wisdom decided, "Hey, maybe we should save a couple of these pigeons so we can rebuild the flock." As usual, old mankind had shot himself in the foot again. Two handsome, lovely birds, handpicked by the Blue Ribbon Committee for this noble undertaking, would have been a tad more useful if an ornithologist had been consulted. The pair of Passenger Pigeons billed and cooed their lives away in the Cincinnati Zoo in 1914. Betty and I thought the Taxidermist did a fine job. We saw the two male birds in a bell jar in a glass cabinet at the Zoo. Live and learn.

BEE HAVE, SWEETY

In later years, Dad could remember a barrel stave factory near the Brown-Johnson County line. Since the market demanded oak staves, most of the virgin oak trees were stripped from the hills for the stave factory. Hard to say how many barrels of Kentucky's finest sippin's were aged in Indiana oak. Most of the hemlock and black locust were saved and used as rail fences because the posts and rails did not rot as quickly as some of the other trees. Black locust is a tough hardwood. Your axe better be good and sharp or you will be plinking all day trying to fell one black locust tree. Black locusts have short, stubby thorns that are needle sharp. The real treat is the big, sweet-smelling white blossoms that attract every sweet-loving critter to dip its proboscis into those deep natural sugary wells.

Think hot biscuits slathered with fresh-churned butter and locust honey just knifed off that light tender wax comb. Don't get sucked into one of those gimmicky, "You can't tell it's not butter," concoctions. The only reason you can't tell is your olfactory nerves are on vacation. Shame on you!

Here is a misnomer: Honey Locust Tree. A bee would die of old age perched up in this tree waiting for honey. More than likely, if he isn't careful, he'll get impaled on one of the three-pronged, three-inch thorns that grow on the tree's branches and trunk. Just to get it done quickly, if cutting a honey locust, the axe should be sharp, but this tree is not a plinker. They cut rather easily. I cleared several when we moved to our circa-1920 farm house.

IN SUMMARY

THEN AND NOW

As I reflect on the stories shared here, I have a good feeling about what I learned during my childhood and the years that followed. Given that our make-up draws from genetics and our environment, I couldn't lose. Sherman A. Nail and Mary Alice Burgett-Nail were, in my view, exemplary parents in every way. My mother was the most caring and compassionate person I ever met. My every memory of her evokes thoughts of deep-seated love. I noticed very early on that she not only made me feel very special, she worked at making everyone she encountered feel that way. Even the hobos who made their way from the train tracks to our back door knew that the lady of our house would never turn them away hungry. And that was during the depression era when money and food were very scarce.

Dad was a teacher on many levels. During the day, Monday through Saturday, I learned the elements of business at the *Nail and Company* store. I saw, first-hand, that hard work, a pleasant disposition, and a quest for continuous improvement were key components for success in the marketplace. Family values were consistently demonstrated at home during the evenings. And while we never missed church on Sundays, our faith formation was by no means limited to that one day each week.

I was so impressed with Mother and Dad's sterling example that I always wanted to emulate them. The influence of my brothers and sisters and the general citizenry model that emerged from the St. Paul, Indiana community added to an already-strong base.

What I learned from Sherman and Mary Alice has always served me well. And it served my brothers and sisters equally well. But when I see the impact that my parents' example has had—and continues to have—on subsequent generations, I feel exceptionally proud. My nieces and nephews have consistently lived out the virtues I first saw in my parents. Their sons and daughters have followed suit. Indeed, the behavior I have recently observed in the young adults and children of our family confirms that my parents built a strong enough foundation to endure the test of time.

GOING FORWARD

In closing, I appeal to the members of all our families—Nail(e), Judy, Steiner, and Wolverton (and their extended families)—to continue the rich tradition. There is no better way to honor my parents (your grandparents, great-grandparents, etc.) than to carry their values forward. In this weary and mixed-up world, our family has the formula to maintain a very high standard. All we must do is to build on the excellent base that has been provided. Hold the baton tightly and pass it on carefully. It is as simple as following the examples of your parents and grandparents— Leon, Adrian, Doris, Evelyn, Marian, James, and yours truly—who had the enviable privilege of learning from two of the world's best parents, Sherman A. and Mary Alice Nail.

Printed in the United States
By Bookmasters